Praise for Young, Gifted

This brings together much of the material that David has collected over his long career in gifted education. The anecdotes, examples of children's work and humourous touches that make his presentations so popular, are all here. His warm and patriarchal voice comes through strongly and as the reader, you know that this author is someone who cares very much about G&T children getting a fair deal. To be gifted and bored is indeed, a travesty.

The components one would expect of any useful book about teaching able children are all here: identifying gifts and talents and looking out for under-achievers; making good provision; paying attention to self-esteem; nurturing gifts and talents in the early years; and 'a few words on parenting'. All is presented in a very concise and accessible format; and easy to dip into.

G&T coordinators and leading teachers will find much to support their work in school, especially in terms of providing CPD for colleagues. The examples of 'celebrity' individuals who were late developers: 'Albert Einstein was four years old before he could speak and seven before he could read ...'; and those castigated by their teachers as 'indolent and illiterate' (Roald Dahl) can bring an extra (enjoyable) dimension to any training you are planning, helping to get colleagues 'on side'. More than this, there are practical resources that will help teachers in their identification of, and provision for, able learners.

Higher order thinking skills, problem solving and creativity are at the heart of good G&T provision, and teachers are exhorted to plan for their inclusion in all lessons. 'Eight great strategies', sections on practical approaches to differentiation and a consideration of questioning skills are all designed to help them in that quest.

Dr Linda Evans, Editor of *G&T Update*

In the world of education, David George is one of a handful of people who truly understands what it means to be gifted and talented. Much has been written and even more spoken about the subject. Yet, our inability to identify gifted children and what to do with them once we have done so is startling.

At last, a book which champions young people of exceptional creativity and talent, who possess the ability to answer old questions and tackle old problems in new ways. That is precisely what David George achieves in his new book. It is long overdue.

Sir John Jones, Writer, Presenter and Educational Consultant

I found this short book revelatory. It sets out very clearly how a large number of children have potential for higher achievement and creativity, but often react with inattention and even antisocial behaviour in contemporary school environments. I suddenly understood why my son gets average marks in class, but occasionally top marks in exams! In well written chapters it sets out how to identify these gifted and talented children, and how to understand, teach, support and parent them. This is referenced to current government educational policy and school practice. I believe schools that enthusiastically pursue a special policy for these children, and work creatively with them, will see spectacular and rewarding results. In this way we can equip a generation with the capabilities needed in the twenty-first century.

Professor Philip Sugarman, Chief Executive, St Andrew's Healthcare

Dr David George has written another excellent book which stands out from similar books on the market. The emphasis is on the crucial early years, the importance of parenting and raising self-esteem. The book is very readable with many practical ideas, charts and tables for busy teachers.

As usual David's book is written with humour and great humanity. He is passionate about education and has a genuine love of children.

Now that 'gifted education' has been cut by the government we must not let the issue be sidelined. This supportive book helps the reader to focus on this issue. The future of each child, and the country, is at stake.

Richard Y. McNulty, Retired Primary School Head Teacher and Inspector

The ability to think is without doubt the most important skill for schools of te twenty-first century to develop and nurture in our pupils. Who knows what the world will expect and require of our current pupils when they complete their compulsory education. What is certain is that they will need to be able to think for themselves and to think creatively. This is David George's philosophy and spur for this book; another, which will be welcomed by teachers, parents and carers alike. David George, as always, writes with conviction and offers both theory and practice.

Honing the skills of thinking does not just happen, not even amongst the most gifted and talented children in our schools, who, if not challenged will become bored and often challenging. George argues cogently that best practice and provision for the gifted and talented enhances the education of all children, and that it is the responsibility of schools to have identification strategies. He makes it clear that there is no quick fix for best provision for the young, gifted and bored, but offers a variety of multidimensional approaches to identification and many ideas for enriching, extending and differentiating the curriculum for pupils of all ages. The latter point is worth emphasising as teachers, and indeed parents and carers, of children of all ages will find this a must read if they are committed to nurturing their charge's thinking abilities and win back the hearts, minds and brains of able, but underachieving, pupils.

In essence, a readable book, written with clarity and deploying evidence that demonstrates George's real enthusiasm for developing pupils' thinking and that his insights and understanding of pupils remain firmly rooted in his regular engagement with pupils in schools across the country.

Elizabeth Garner, Head, Forest Preparatory School

Young, Gifted and Bored by David George is a practical insight into the mind of the gifted and talented child or young person. It gives both teaching staff and parents alike practical tools to help identify, assess and nurture the young minds of those with high learning potential. The book's emphasis is on the importance of parents and teachers working together to ensure that the young and gifted are definitely not bored but are effectively challenged in the classroom and beyond. It is an easy read for anyone working with children and young people, particularly those who are looking to explore other reasons for underachievement.

Denise Yates, Chief Executive,
The National Association for Gifted Children (NAGC)

Anyone who has experienced David George's training courses has come to expect an inspirational tour de force in working with the most able. His new book *Young Gifted and Bored* does no less in print. It is a world away from dry pedagogical theory and deeply embedded in sparkling realism which every teacher will relate to and can learn from. He manages to combine instruction with entertainment and amusement. No teacher will read this book and not feel enlivened and emboldened in their teaching: Dr George ought to be available on prescription. A lifetime of real chalkface experience and expert knowledge of our most amazing young people, and how to respond to their needs, are woven into this remarkable and highly readable book.

Matthew Judd, Second Master, Haberdashers' Aske's Boys' School,
former Principal, Mander Portman Woodward College

David creates a clear and readable context for the education of gifted and talented young people. We are educating our children for an unknown and uncertain future and David's short book allows us to explore and extend a range of approaches that will stretch those most able children and improve the provision for all. David's warm and open approach underpins much of this work and is blended with a sharp focus of how teacher's can change their classroom practice. Parents, decision makers and teachers will find practical strategies and instruments to review their provision and ensure their children remain fully engaged!

Chris Grimshaw, International Consultant

Young Gifted
and Bored

Young Gifted and Bored

David George

edited by Ian Gilbert

Crown House Publishing Ltd
www.crownhouse.co.uk
www.crownhousepublishing.com

First published by
Crown House Publishing Ltd
Crown Buildings, Bancyfelin, Carmarthen, Wales, SA33 5ND, UK
www.crownhouse.co.uk
and
Crown House Publishing Company LLC
6 Trowbridge Drive, Suite 5, Bethel, CT 06801, USA
www.crownhousepublishing.com

British Library of Cataloguing-in-Publication Data
A catalogue entry for this book is available
from the British Library.

10-digit ISBN 184590680-2
13-digit ISBN 978-184590680-1

LCCN 2010937325

Printed and bound in the UK by
Bell & Bain Ltd, Glasgow

Foreword

How many times have you heard people tell children – or heard it from your own mouth – that they should never 'blow their own trumpet'? Or become 'too big for their boots'? Or let that success 'go to their head'? How often have we watched people rise to the top of their field exploiting whatever gift or talent they have, only to relish their sudden demise and fall from public grace? Apart from the sports pages, why else would the Sunday papers exist?

Maybe it's a peculiarly British trait, this notion of not really wanting people to be better than we are and, when they are, to resent them for it. Perhaps it's related to a class thing, where we have been taught to 'know our station' in life, to know exactly where we stand in the John Cleese, Ronnie Barker, Ronnie Corbett line-up (and if you don't recognise that reference have a look here http://www.youtube.com/watch?v=woDUsGSMwZY and then use the clip as a teaching resource for your next PSHE lesson).

Or perhaps it originated in the 1960s and the push for a comprehensive system of education where the 'grammar school/secondary modern'; 'brains/good with your hands' divide no longer reigned and we decided that all children were equal and all deserved the same opportunities, something that somehow came to mean that all children are the same and all deserve the same. Maybe this is why the notion of gifted and talented children has caused such resentment and consternation in so many members of the teaching profession for whom the idea of some children being 'better' than others seems to fit so uncomfortably with their egalitarian ideals.

Yet, as any of you who grew up with an elder brother will know, 'equal' and 'fair' aren't the same things at all.

Everyone has an equal right to be educated and by educated I mean educated in the truest sense. To have the very best of what each child brings to school brought out and developed as far as is possible as part of that child's journey to adulthood. Whatever 'subject' we teach we are a teacher of children and it is our moral, ethical and professional responsibility to act on that daily in helping all children start to become all they can be. Yet education is not the same as being 'schooled', a process by which children are trained to pass tests that are important in so much they measure a country's ability to get children to pass these tests, regardless of their ability to be creative or brave or honourable or to be able to think deeply or even think for themselves.

Which brings us to talent and also to motivation Equality of rights does not mean equality of ability. Equality of rights does not mean I have to use those rights. Everybody can join the school football team but not everyone does. Everybody can enter the school library (or 'learning resource centre' as they are now known, although with the current changes in the direction of UK education they will probably soon be called 'libraries' again, with books in Latin) but some children wouldn't be seen dead in there, unless they were hiding. Not everyone wants to be part of the school musical, despite the best efforts of *Glee* and anyway, a bit like public speaking and being on TV, just because you can do it doesn't mean you should.

Which brings us to dopamine. If you are looking for ways to engage learners and fire them up to learn effectively, enthusiastically and enjoyably then this neurochemical really is 'teacher's little helper'. Dopamine is a naturally occurring neurotransmitter that is linked to memory, to learning and to attention. What is the secret to firing the learning brain with the right amount of dopamine to make learning almost effortless? Reward and the anticipation of reward. In other words, doing something that you get a kick out of doing and also knowing you are about to do something that you get a kick out of doing.

Which brings us, finally, to the title of this book, 'Young, Gifted and Bored', a name that springs from Dr David George's pioneering work in education for many years and from his recent focus on what are known as 'gifted underachievers'. These are the young people in our classrooms who have so much to offer, who fit the best current definition of 'gifted and talented' but whose energies are not tapped by current teaching practice, whose time is spent avoiding using those talents or using them – and getting their dopamine fix

– to create disruption and mayhem in the classroom. What David is suggesting is that if we seek to understand their natures and their needs better, if we adapt the way we work with these young people in our schools and homes, if we seek to let them exploit their strengths, if we challenge them to be better than they are, even if that means being better than the young person sitting next to them or, heaven forefend, better than we are, then maybe we can rescue them from their own boredom and frustration with a school system that is failing them not because it is too hard but because it is too easy.

There is phrase which David uses that can be traced back to John F. Kennedy, if not further, and that is relevant for all teachers who perhaps struggle with the very concept of gifted and talented children. It is that 'a rising tide lifts all ships'. In other words, take up David's challenge and stretch yourself to stretch the young, gifted and bored in your care. In doing so, *all* your learners will benefit and learn to discover the pleasure of successfully blowing whatever trumpet they have.

Ian Gilbert,
January 2011

Acknowledgements

I would like to express my warmest thanks to numerous friends and colleagues who have supported me during the writing of this book: Ian Gilbert of Independent Thinking, who invited me to write the book in the first place, for his inspiration and for writing the Foreword; Tim Dracup from the Department for Children, Schools and Families and Ian Warwick from London Gifted and Talented for their encouragement and helpful discussions; Corinne Maskell for her patience in typing the script so ably; Crown House Publishing for their thorough editing and generous support; and to my lovely wife and family who are always there for me.

Thank you to the numerous teachers, parents and children who have contributed in many ways through discussions and anecdotes, and for permission to use their ideas and materials. I continue to learn from them.

Lastly, my apologies to those who I may have inadvertently left out or not acknowledged in the text.

Contents

Introduction

Introduction

The principal aim of education in schools should be to create young people who are capable of being creative thinkers – who can do things to make the world a better place, not merely repeating what others have done before them.

Meeting the needs of gifted and talented children has become a topic of widespread debate. A great deal of time, energy and money has been spent on children with other special needs whereas the requirements of children of high ability have been relatively neglected. However, during the last ten years the Department for Children, Schools and Families (DCSF – but now the Department for Education) have begun to put substantial sums of money into gifted and talented education. Alongside the more vigorous and frequent monitoring of schools that has come about through Ofsted inspections, the focus in this area has sharpened at last.

I maintain that many, though not all, gifted and talented children have special needs and problems, not the least of which is that they are so often bored by the education system in which they find themselves: lessons which don't stretch them, teachers who don't understand them, peers who hold them back. Frustrated, they often simply switch off or, worse, start to make trouble as a way of adding some spice to their day. Yet they also have exceptional, sometimes immense, talents to offer. We owe it to them and to society to cultivate their abilities to help prepare tomorrow's leaders and talent. These children are a precious natural resource and one that we must not squander. Indeed, the survival of the human species owes much to one characteristic – a capacity for creative problem solving. This ability to find new answers to difficulties remains a vital one. A major objective of education for these children is to recognize and foster their unique abilities. Unfortunately, the pursuit of this and related objectives is often plagued with confusion, misconceptions, doubtful assumptions, exaggerated claims and a lack of communication.

..dertake numerous courses for gifted and talented children and often .ave frank discussions with these outstanding students. A recurrent theme is that many of them (40 per cent) are bored and others say they already know what is being taught (30 per cent). I argue strongly that repetition, regurgitation and revision for these children does them a great disservice and leads to them becoming bored and turned off from school. And all the time the clock is ticking as they while away their days without being stretched or sometimes even noticed.

It is the right of all children to go as far and as fast as they can along every dimension of the school curriculum without any brakes being put on them. Therefore, every child is entitled to the best programme, the most attentive care and the greatest love and respect.

Guy Claxton (2008) states that most people would agree that the only thing we can say with any confidence about the year 2025 is there is not much we can say about it with any confidence. Of course we want to give young people the knowledge and attitudes we value. The trouble is most societies are now a jumble of different sorts of 'we', each casting their shadow in a different direction. The only sensible role for education is to get young people ready to cope well with complexity, uncertainty and ambiguity. It is estimated that children in primary school today will possibly live to the age of 100 and have at least six jobs during their career. With such a future in mind we need to turn out flexible generalists because the world is changing so fast.

And it is the very process by which we can do this that will make school a whole lot more engaging for gifted yet bored students. But who are they? According to official DCSF guidelines (see Dracup, 2009) they are children and young people with one or more abilities developed to a level significantly ahead of a year group, or with a potential to develop those abilities. They estimate that this amounts to: 820,000 individuals in schools, an estimated 140,000 in post-16 settings and a target to identify one million gifted and talented students for the year 2010.

This means:

- A national gifted and talented population aged 4 to 19.

- A gifted and talented population in *all* primary and secondary schools and colleges.

- Top 5 per cent nationally aged 11 to 19 determined using published criteria (otherwise schools identify these children themselves).

- A marker, not necessarily permanent, that the learner needs extra support – *if* we are to challenge them and help them to re-engage.

If the DCSF/DoE is ready to admit that there is such a thing as a 'gifted and talented' student, schools are sometimes less so. However, here is my own personal eight-point rationale as to why schools must address this issue. Feel free to use it with any of your colleagues who bemoan the behaviour of that clever yet disaffected child, but who refuses to acknowledge that the problem can be addressed through a whole-school focus on the gifted and talented.

1. It is every child's right to go as far and as fast along every dimension of the school curriculum – 'excellence for all' as most schools like to say in their prospectus. We must support schools in meeting the needs of *all* their learners, something that falls very much under the 'personalization' banner.

2. Some children have special needs – supporting disadvantaged learners means narrowing the achievement gap.

3. There is evidence from HM Inspectorate of Education and Ofsted that if a school has a gifted and talented coordinator and work is done to identify and work with gifted and talented children then *all* children benefit. This is a key driver for whole-school improvement. 'A rising tide raises all ships' as they say.

4. The world needs these children – they are the brains of the future and have immense talent to give to society.

5. Aptitude is equally distributed across all social classes but opportunities are not. We must identify and nurture all talents in our schools in order to narrow achievement gaps.

6. Education should be a gateway to a more equal society.

7. There is a suggestion (largely anecdotal) that if we do not provide for these children then some engage in antisocial behaviour beyond school.

8. There is evidence that some children underachieve. Some coast deliberately; these are the young, gifted and bored.

In addition to this rationale, other benefits include: improvements in learner achievement/performance; more effective teaching, learning and whole-school support; less underachievement by disadvantaged learners; more and better external learning opportunities; better schools; improved support for parents and educators; and enhanced social mobility and national competitiveness.

From April 2011, however, there will be no more national strategies. Instead, the Department of Education will establish frameworks for quality assured providers and the opportunity for leading schools to support their peers.

What does all this mean? It is now, more than ever, down to individual schools and individual teachers – down to you – to drive the movement forward, to work out priorities and come up with your own high quality approaches to bring the best out of your gifted and talented learners.

Childhood isn't what it used to be: it will never be the same again

Children are able to learn more outside the classroom as they are only in school for 17 per cent of their working life over a year.

The greatest influence on our children are parents, peer group and the environment. This is why they learn so much outside school; that is, education does not stop at the school gates. The diagram below gives evidence for this and more. This is why I suggest to teachers that a school day never ends with a full stop, always a question mark. Therefore they have time for homework!

Children are able to learn more outside school than at any other time in human history

Children are maturing physically and emotionally much earlier than ever before

Expectations of what children can understand and do have risen and continue to rise rapidly

Schools, and what they provide, can radically inhibit children's natural abilities in learning as well as extending them

We know more about how children learn than ever before

Educational standards in literacy and numeracy are higher than they have ever been (especially at higher levels)

Parents are better placed to help their children learn than ever before

To help you make a start, here is a gifted and talented quality standard model that I know many schools have found useful. If a school can achieve all of this then they are an exemplary model for others to emulate.

Gifted and talented quality standards for busy teachers

G&T is not an add-on but an integral part of teaching and learning

Effective G&T provision is effective provision for all – all benefit

Collect examples of challenges (e.g. lateral thinking puzzles or problem-solving activities) that can be used for a Challenge Box in the classroom

Consider alternative ways to record work (e.g. photos, mind-mapping, charts, tapes)

Distribute responsibility for G&T among all your staff. Establish a link teacher in each subject department to create a G&T team

Celebrate achievement in all areas

Set challenging targets. Focus on what the student needs to do to reach the next level

Give pupils a wide variety of opportunities – make contact with your local museums and artists, etc.

Use marking to indicate next steps

Homework does not always have to be written!

Best example of differentiation

Use websites such as http://nrich.maths.org to stimulate and challenge your G&T learners

Encourage pupils to enter national competitions

Give **HOTS** (Higher Order Thinking Skills) not **MOTS** (More of The Same)

G&Ts should do less and learn more

Give pupils the opportunity to discuss challenging questions

Have a five minute slot in every staff meeting to discuss G&T issues

Keep a portfolio of exemplary work in all subjects

Include higher order skills and questions in your planning

I suggest that the monopoly schools have had on the education industry is breaking down fast as we now know much more about how children learn, and therefore how teachers should teach. Learning is becoming less school contained and some schools will need to decide what they can do that is unique to them and which cannot easily be achieved elsewhere. I predict that schools will become more social and sport orientated because most of the knowledge base can be acquired elsewhere (e.g. at home or on the internet). As one child recently said to me: 'I am only going to school until it becomes available as an iPhone app!'

All of the above have serious implications for bringing the best out of our gifted and talented children.

This book will discuss the problems of definitions, offer a variety of multidimensional approaches to identification and, more importantly for these children, provide lots of ideas about how busy teachers can enrich, extend and differentiate the curriculum to win back the hearts, minds and brains of the able but underachieving students in their classrooms.

It is my hope that all of you who care about gifted individuals will find much that will help you to discover the excitement, challenge and pleasure of being with these special children as we share with them the process of growing up. The waste of human potential is tragic for our communities, for the world, but most especially for the child. The concerto never written, the scientific discovery never made, the political compromise never found – they all carry a heavy cost. Thomas Gray notes this loss in his 'Elegy Written in a Country Churchyard': 'Full many a flower is born to blush unseen / And waste its sweetness on the desert air'.

If children are to reach their considerable potential then the model below makes clear those who will make it. These students are obviously very able, some are very creative; but they all have to work hard.

Maximum potential

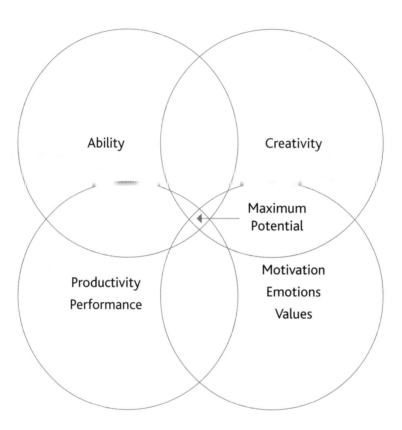

Ability

Creativity

Maximum
Potential

Productivity
Performance

Motivation
Emotions
Values

The United Kingdom has a huge number of Nobel prizewinners who are creative thinkers – second only in number to the United States. However, they all worked extremely hard. Thomas Edison, for example, one of the greatest inventors of all time, said: 'Genius is one per cent inspiration, ninety-nine per cent perspiration.' Mozart had practised on the piano for two and a half thousand hours before he was 6 and had an exceptional work rate. He was actively encouraged by his father Leopold who wanted to turn him into a concert pianist by the age of 6, and he did!

However, the most important aspect of the Maximum Potential model is motivation/emotion/values. If students are not keen to learn, and if they are not excited about going to school, then they will not achieve their potential. Add to that the need to develop their emotional intelligence – the ability to get on with ourselves as well as each other – and the importance of providing children with a decent values education becomes critical. For more information on values education please see Chapter 4 and *The Little Book of Values* by Julie Duckworth.

Chapter 1
Gifted Underachievers

Chapter 1
Gifted Underachievers

The only rational way of educating is to be an example. If one cannot help it, a warning example.

Albert Einstein

Gifted underachievers present a particular challenge to the teacher. They are frequently difficult to identify because there can often be little in the student's work that gives a clue to the high underlying ability. Recognition is often dependent upon the skill of teachers in spotting the warning signs of the young, gifted and bored such as those on the following list:

1. Apparently bored.

2. Fluent orally but poor in written work.

3. Friendly with older children and adults.

4. Absorbed in private world.

5. Outwardly self-sufficient.

6. Excessively self-critical.

7. Anxious and may feel rejected by family.

8. Possibly emotionally unstable.

9. Hostile towards authority – anti-school.

10. Quick thinking.

11. Doesn't know how to learn academically.

12. Aspirations too low for aptitudes.

13. Does not set own goals.

14. Does not think ahead.

15. Poor performance in tests but asks creative and searching questions.

16. Thinks in abstract terms.

17. Enjoys playing with language.

18. High level work has deteriorated over time.

19. Impatient with slower learners.

20. Can be creative when motivated.

21. Inconsistent work.

22. Lack of concentration.

23. Daydreaming.

24. Disorganization.

25. Non-completion of assignments.

26. Poor study habits.

Of course history is full of people who underachieve. These creative and imaginative people are often not recognized by their contemporaries. In fact, often they are not recognized in school by their teachers either. Consider some of the following examples:

- **Albert Einstein** – He was 4 years old before he could speak and 7 before he could read. He became the gifted 'synthesizer' of the time/space continuum. He was often caught daydreaming and dreamt up the theory of relativity over three days.

- **Isaac Newton** – One of our greatest scientists did poorly in high school.

- **Ludwig van Beethoven** – He was told by his music teacher that as a composer he was hopeless and would never make a good musician.

- **Winston Churchill** – He failed the equivalent of the 11+ examination.

- **Dame Alicia Markova** – Was taken to the doctor because she had flat feet. Guess what he recommended? Yes, ballet dancing.

- **Abraham Lincoln** – He entered the Black Hawk War as a captain and came out as a private!

- **David Bellamy** – His school report at 15 stated that he is a 'good fellow' and 'maturing well', but is 'academically useless'. He is now very proud of that comment!

- **Oprah Winfrey** – Came from a very poor household, had with a difficult childhood and became pregnant at 16.

- **Noël Coward** – When he was 2 a doctor pronounced that his brain was much in advance of his body and advised that he should be left very quiet, that all his curls should be cut off and he was to go to no parties!

See if your students can match the well-known personality with the comments made about them at school:

What the school reports said ...

1.	'Is a constant trouble to everybody and is always in some scrape or other'	Jeremy Paxman
2.	'Would be a very good pupil if she lived in this world'	Roald Dahl
3.	'She has no staying power'	John Lennon
4.	'Indolent and illiterate'	Eric Morecombe
5.	'He has glaring faults and they have certainly glared at us this term'	Judi Dench
6.	'This boy will never get anywhere in life'	Winston Churchill
7.	'Fairly responsible adult who might go far'	Stephen Fry
8.	'He must learn tact without losing his outspokenness'	Margaret Thatcher

Can you match the comments to the well known person? Answers can be found on page 20.

All of these people were probably identified as underachievers or misfits at school. The phenomenon of underachieving is puzzling and challenging; puzzling in its complexity and challenging in its significance of the reversal of this costly syndrome.

Underachievement is a discrepancy between a child's school performance and some index of his or her actual ability (a diminution of grades, quality work by middle years) and this shows itself by disenchantment with school.

I carried out a major piece of research by questionnaire, addressed to head teachers, teachers, parents, inspectors and children (see George, 1997). It is a good exercise to undertake in a staff meeting or to give out to the Parent Teacher Association, and makes us all think carefully about what constitutes 'achievement'.

Exercise for teachers and parents

What is achievement?

Read through the descriptions of achievement listed below and rank them in order of importance, giving the most important number 1, the next important number 2 and so on.

- Attainment and test scores.

- Public exam results.

- Expected public exam results.

- Continuous assessment scores.

- Continuous assessment feedback.

- 'In the top set'.

- Teacher assessment of pupil's learning and progress.

- Pupil's assessment of learning and progress.

- Opportunities for pupils to use what they know or can do.

- Opportunities for pupils to have a broad education.

- Personal development, e.g. confidence.

- Any other (please state).

> Now do the same with these processes that affect achievement:
>
> ■ Choice for pupil.
>
> ■ Relevance of the curriculum for pupils.
>
> ■ Breadth of the curriculum.
>
> ■ Teacher's style of instruction.
>
> ■ Teacher's clear presentation.
>
> ■ Pupil's relationship with teacher.
>
> ■ Teacher's expectation of individual pupils.
>
> ■ Behaviour of pupils in class.
>
> ■ Quality of school staff relationships.
>
> ■ Quality of resources and environment.
>
> ■ Quality of teacher's relationship with parents.
>
> ■ Quality of school's relationship with parents.
>
> ■ Any other (please state).

I was perturbed by the number of parents and children who scored from the top down (achievement is getting good exam results, being in the top set, etc.) whereas most teachers scored from the bottom up.

Let us now pause and consider what we mean by the words *abilities, attainment* and *achievement*.

---

1 Winston Churchill	4 Roald Dahl	7 John Lennon
2 Judi Dench	5 Stephen Fry	8 Jeremy Paxman
3 Margaret Thatcher	6 Eric Morecombe	

Abilities	Attainment	Achievement
The capacity to learn in a subject or sport – not age related.	An educational term related to gaining competence in single steps in a whole process.	A commonly held and well understood concept.
An innate propensity to learn quickly and easily.	Gaining results in a test of specific ability.	Using what a person knows or can do.
The power or capacity to do something well.	The result of a test or task-based assessment.	Using skills, knowledge and understanding to achieve a goal which has social and/or cultural recognition.
A competency acquired as a result of teaching.	Accomplishments by hard work.	
Being clever at something.		

To help you understand the difference, let us consider the great Dame Kelly Holmes. Kelly had enormous *ability* and worked consistently hard in order to get to the 2000 Olympic Games in Sydney. Her *attainment* was to win two gold medals, and we should never forget the expression on her face as she crossed the line. Now her *achievement* is that she is giving so much time to black girl athletes in encouraging them to train for success in athletics.

Once we have identified underachievement in our gifted students what can we do about it? For a start, here is my seven-step cure for underachievement:

1. Assessment – The first step in the underachievement reversal process is an assessment that involves the cooperation of educational psychologists, teachers and parents.

2. Communication – Communication between parents and teachers is an important component in the cure for underachievers. This should include a discussion of assessed abilities and achievements as well as

formal and informal evaluations of the child's expression of dependence or dominance in order to avoid reinforcing these problems. This may again involve an educational psychologist or at least a wise school counsellor, form tutor or group leader.

3. High expectations – Changing expectations is often difficult because sometimes parents and teachers have low expectations of children owing to various factors. However, it is important to underachieving students that parents and teachers are honestly able to express belief in their potential for greater achievement.

4. Role model identification – A critical turning point for the underachieving child is the discovery of a role model for them to identify with.

5. Correction of deficiencies – Showing the child where they are underachieving and how they could improve their performance. This could be undertaken by a form tutor or mentor.

6. Reinforcement – The behaviour discussed in Step 1 will identify some of the areas where reinforcement at home and school will help the underachieving student. These may take the form of rewards which are meaningful to the child and should be within the value system of parents and child, as well as being within the capabilities of teachers to administer.

7. Patient, dedicated, warm and encouraging support from both teachers and parents – we need gifted teachers for gifted children.

Butler-Por (1987) concludes that we should adopt a multidimensional approach to the problems of underachieving children, providing an appropriate educational environment in the classroom and utilizing teaching methods capable of answering children's needs. These can contribute towards reversing underachievement in young people of all ability levels.

Knowing how to spot the young, gifted and bored is one thing; but the starting point is understanding where to look. In fact, as we learn more about the characteristics of gifted and talented children, we find that a significant proportion of them have been overlooked. These students demonstrate their abilities only if they are given the circumstances and opportunities that might enable them to emerge.

Students with 'hidden talents' could well be found in the following groups:

■ Those from low socio-economic backgrounds.

■ Female students who, for example, are under-represented in higher levels of maths and science.

■ Male students who under-participate in languages and humanities.

■ Students with learning difficulties or specific disabilities.

■ Students with poor self-concept or inhibiting social and/or economic problems.

■ Students from homes where there are low expectations and/or negative attitudes towards schools and teachers.

■ Students from ethnic minority groups with a different culture and language.

■ Students whose education has been disrupted for various reasons, such as family mobility.

■ Students who have particularly divergent thinking and are non-conforming.

After identification comes assessment. Effective evaluation is a means of motivating, developing and recognizing student achievement and self-esteem and of providing constructive feedback to all concerned. Teachers continually assess children by a variety of methods and not just by testing.

Here is a useful five-point school assessment policy you can employ:

1. **The aims of assessment:**

   ● To involve students in review and target-setting to maximize encouragement, motivation and progress.

   ● To provide an accurate representation of student achievement for effective use in setting student targets and evaluating and planning teaching programmes.

   ● To provide regular and accurate information for students, parents, teachers and governors.

   ● To celebrate success and avoid underachievement.

2. **The assessment process:**

   ● Is an integral part of the school year reflecting the requirements of the National Curriculum and other syllabuses.

   ● Is a manageable part of the learning process.

   ● Takes account of differentiation.

   ● Is founded in knowledge of the criteria for assessment and routes of progression.

   ● Is based upon understanding of the assessment procedures.

   ● Is founded in student self-assessment incorporating reflecting, review, recording and target-setting.

3. **The assessment structure:**

    ● Is anchored in agreed departmental policy in which there is standardization of approach based on:

        ● Departmental portfolios of exemplars of agreed levels.

        ● Clearly defined marking criteria and comments.

        ● Accurate and easy-to-use assessment guidelines.

4. **The assessment recording system:**

    ● Involves teachers and students in a manageable, accessible structure.

    ● Gives a clear and accurate indicator of student attainment.

    ● Records achievements and levels to indicate progression from year to year, key stage to key stage and school to school.

    ● Responds to internal school and external educational demands.

5. **The assessment reporting process:**

    ● Should be regular, rapid, clear, concise, constructive, informative, honest and accurate.

    ● Should identify strengths and weaknesses.

    ● Should involve and be valued by students and parents for its effective, encouraging and personal content.

We must create an 'ethos of achievement' in our schools by working in partnership with parents and teachers. The following steps were strongly recommended by a group of secondary school teachers in a workshop during one of my in-service training courses.

1. All pupils know that they are valued and cared for.

2. Teamwork ethos cultivated and fostered.

3. Celebration of successes (e.g. academic, sporting, drama, caring) through assemblies, tutor groups, commendations, letters home, etc.

4. Emphasis on the positive; the negative is suppressed.

5. Good attendance is rewarded. Pupils value coming to school; we leave them wanting more.

6. Enrichment of the curriculum by extra-curricular activities. Pupils have lots of opportunities outside the classroom, if they know about them.

7. Valued rewards system.

8. Pupils given responsibility at home and school.

9. Pupils contribute to the development of the school, e.g. school council members.

10. Entering/winning competitions – local and national.

11. Sense of identity and purpose – school is well led. Parents, staff and Pupils are informed and consulted. Whole-team approach – parents are good role models.

12. Take risks – make it work!

13. Have a system in place to recognize underachievement – monitoring/ encouragement.

14. School environment is comfortable, creative and pleasant.

15. Pupils are trusted; excellent relationships between pupils and staff.

How we get it wrong (Part 1): The Year 7 Bermuda Triangle of achievement

There has been great concern for some time that there is a dip in pupil performance in Years 7 and 8, compared to Year 6 in primary school. The following are some of the reasons given by teachers:

■ Inadequate curriculum continuity between primary and secondary. If we truly believe that children learn so much in the crucial early years, it is vitally important that secondary colleagues take notice of what learning young people have acquired in their first eleven years of life before entering Year 7 at the secondary stage.

■ Unsatisfactory progression in teaching and learning.

■ Methods of teaching dramatically changes. There is evidence of much repetition, regurgitation and revision. We should actively encourage Year 6 teachers to talk to Year 7 teachers and give colleagues a succinct summary of a child's ability, interests, hobbies and so on, on entering the secondary phase.

■ Over-protectiveness in new schools spills over into classrooms academically ('Fresh start'). It is common practice in many secondary schools to teach what students already know, to test them again rather than finding out what they already know (i.e. in the first eleven years of life) and let them move on smoothly.

■ Some children feel lost in a 'big' school – they miss their Circle Time and attachment to a secure base.

■ The onset of adolescence – this is a huge factor and it is therefore understandable that Years 8 and 9 are the most difficult to teach.

In short, we need much better liaison between primary and secondary schools to inform future planning.

How we get it wrong (Part 2): Boys aren't girls aren't boys

There are significant differences between the way girls and boys behave and learn, which can become particularly problematic during adolescence. The case has been made convincingly for single-sex education; boys and girls, if they are taught separately, achieve higher, there are fewer behaviour problems and less showing off.

Girls	Boys
Greater maturity at 11 years.	Want to do things quickly.
Progressing in reading, verbal and non-verbal.	Read less.
More likely to work on-task and set high standards for themselves.	Do not take much care with presentation.
More comfortable being reflective – analysing and expressing feelings.	Prefer experiential learning style.
Like to sit and write.	Like 'a good laugh'. Tend to opt for open discussion and physical involvement.
Prefer reflective and extended writing.	Narrower experiences of fiction.
Analysts and reflectors.	Speculators and experimenters.

In addition I believe that boys are more likely to need additional support as for each girl receiving special educational needs support there are seven boys; for each girl with dyslexia there are nine boys and for each girl with Asperger's syndrome there are twenty boys.

How we get it wrong (Part 3): Adolescents aren't people

The significance of *adolescence* lies in the fact that along with *childhood* it provides the foundation for *adulthood*. I firmly believe that the crucial early years are the most important phase. Foundations are laid down by good parenting and/or nurseries by the age of 5 (see Chapter 5): 'Train up a child in the way he should go: and when he is old he will not depart from it' (Proverbs 22:6). Childhood leads into adolescence which is a period of great bodily change with surges in hormones and also is a time of experimentation for young people. The diagram below outlines the changes which lead into adulthood. Parents and teachers need to work in partnership to help teenagers cope with this transitional change in their lives: you have to lose them to keep them.

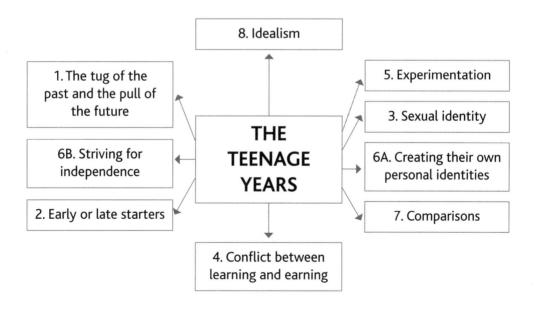

How to get it wrong (Part 4):
Equity vs. excellence

There is a delicate balance when attempting to give all pupils equality of opportunity. For example, we want every child to be able to read but at the same time many gifted children need to be stretched and to show how excellent they can be. Teachers need to be outstanding if they are to enable all pupils to achieve their maximum potential. Teachers need help, excellent resources and the ability to differentiate the curriculum – rather than giving gifted students more of the same work to do.

Equity	Excellence
The identification and education of gifted students merely maintains unequal educational opportunity. Many students from poor families are overlooked.	The new information age will require the best performance from the best students. Gifted students are bored and discouraged from serious study by a lack of challenge.
Inclusion offers the best chance of equalizing access to a superior education.	Inclusion is one sure way to reduce the effort and performance of gifted students.

In short, there are thirteen ways to guarantee success:

1. Teach what you are going to test/assess.

2. Don't make everything as difficult as possible.

3. Never teach things they have failed at before.

4. Don't make it boring.

5. Encourage talking in the classroom/laboratory.

6. Never be negative, always positive.

7. Make your writing, marking, worksheets and board work as legible as you can.

8. Give them plenty of time to do it.

9. Offer rewards for finished work.

10. Give rewards they want or like.

11. Expect them to succeed and be surprised when they fail.

12. Emphasize their strengths and successes, never their weaknesses and mistakes.

13. Don't blame them, their parents or the government – what effect can you have?

A useful starting point for getting it right

Educators can learn a great deal from what children frankly and honestly say to us about themselves as learners. A good survey, which is suitable for all children to undertake, is as follows.

Myself as a learner

Learning is most enjoyable for me when ...

Things I am skilled or good at, as a learner, include ...

My favourite question is ...

I get least out of learning when ...

The thing I would like to change about myself as a learner is ...

The most recent thing I have learnt is ...

The answers to these enquiries can be very revealing and can be helpful in conquering underachievement. See George (1997) for further exercises.

Chapter 2
Identification Strategies

Chapter 2
Identification Strategies

An instrument has been developed in advance of the needs of its possessor.

Alfred Wallace

The preliminary discussion of the young, gifted and bored in this chapter is fundamentally linked with the need to develop identification techniques and procedures which a busy teacher can use in the classroom. We now accept that children can be gifted or talented in various areas so it is not surprising that many different criteria can be used to identify such children. These resources can be categorized into three major areas:

1. Teacher appraisal of their students.

2. The use of weighting scales and checklists.

3. Administration of different types of standardized test.

However, Ofsted report that what they actually observe being used in our schools primarily are test results (Cognitive Abilities Tests (CATs) or Performance Indicators in Primary Schools (PIPS)) and teacher nomination. Unfortunately, appraisals and tests do not always correlate because individual teachers have different standards and, of course, children will rise and fall according to teachers' expectations. Therefore, I want to suggest that we can cast the net much wider. If we do not, we will miss at least 50 per cent of the gifted and talented children in our schools (Freeman, 1991).

The definition that schools have adopted of gifted and talented pupils indicates that these students can possess superior capabilities in several areas, including intellectual/academic, creative, social/leadership and psychomotor skills. Indeed, the specific characteristics of the heterogeneous group known as 'gifted and talented' are numerous and individual pupils might display any combination of these qualities.

Historically, the identification process for gifted and talented children has been stimulated by the desire to gain more information about them in order to deliver an appropriate educational programme; until recently this has meant providing additional enrichment materials. However, there is also a need for teachers and administrators to agree on the type of giftedness being identified. The measures used to screen and identify these students should be compatible with the pupil population and the programme the school wishes to provide. Pupil populations vary enormously depending on ethnicity, parenting and so on. In such cases very specific talents emerge (e.g., dance, languages, sport) so in identification we should cast the net wide. Gifted and talented means much more than an academically able child who produces high quality work.

Teachers should know their children

Good professional educators not only know their children well – especially in primary schools where a teacher may have thirty children for a year; they also involve parents in their holistic education. In secondary schools, however, subject-specific teachers might well teach 200 different children a week and therefore face a bigger challenge in getting to know them all really well.

As a first step, the head teacher and staff should ask themselves the following simple question: Do we have the best possible system for assessing, recording and communicating the needs of each child accurately, and are these records accessible to teachers and passed on from year to year?

A system should be established for the clear recording of pupils' achievements and progress; tracking a child through the day, through the week and through the year is of the utmost importance. One would hope that every staff meeting had an item on the agenda headed 'children of concern', and this would include the gifted underachiever wandering listlessly or destructively through their school career. There should also be a procedure for regular and frequent exchange of information between teachers contributing to the total record.

On page 60 there is a suggested referral form for young, gifted and bored children and a method for recording observations. This should be available to all teachers who would then hand it on to their gifted and talented coordinator (GATCO) and, hopefully between them, make things happen.

There are three principles that a teacher should consider when identifying gifted and talented children:

1. Ensure the process of identification is rooted in an area that the child has been allowed to experience, (e.g. interests like sport, drama and creative subjects).

2. Ensure that the child can express her/himself and listen carefully.

3. Ensure that the process of identification points towards useful developments and extension of the child's work.

The table below provides a summary of eight identification strategies which cast the net widely, so that we do not miss any child who should be on the school register.

How to identify gifted and talented children

Method	Use and limitations
1. Teacher observation	This is essential and the trained teacher should know their children well. However, busy teachers may miss students who do not conform to accepted standards of work or behaviour, who present motivational or emotional problems, those with belligerent or apathetic attitudes or who come from homes which do not share the school's ethos of achievement.
2. Checklists (see below) **General and specific**	These may be useful as an indicator for what to look out for but may not be relevant for individual cases. Remember: checklists can be misleading as it is not always easy to quantify these traits.
3. Intelligence tests (see below)	These can be useful as an initial screen to supplement and counterbalance teacher observations. They may not identify those with motivational or emotional problems, with reading difficulties, from different ethnic/cultural backgrounds or gifted underachievers.
4. Achievement test batteries	These are helpful in providing more detailed information on a wider range of skills, but are subject to the same limitations as group tests. They will not necessarily identify the true abilities of children including aspects such as leadership or social skills.
5. Creativity tests	These may offer a chance to show imagination and divergent thinking in those children overlooked by conventional tests. But they are difficult to assess and time consuming to administer.

Method	Use and limitations
6. Individual intelligence tests	These provide more accurate and reliable information on 'ability to reason' in conventional terms. But they may not indicate how a child will perform in class or predict achievement in individual cases. They are costly in the use of time and can be subject to cultural bias.
7. Nomination	Useful information from parents, peer group and staff to build up a profile.
8. Creative learning environments	The all-important ingredient! Encourage *all* children to explore their talents, exercise their developing capacity to learn and understand and to reach the highest potential of which they are capable (see page 40).

It is essential to provide a creative learning environment in which these exceptional children have the opportunity to show their talents (see the checklists on pages 43-44). Education is changing dramatically because of the learning revolution coupled with the electronic revolution. Regretfully I still see some teachers who do the opposite and provide a non-creative environment. At the heart of a school policy for the gifted and talented, in my view, is that the maximum opportunity should be provided for the learner to take maximum responsibility for developing his or her own learning with the support and encouragement that enables acceleration and fast tracking to take place. Able children should be encouraged to become independent learners so that they make choices about their work, carry out tasks unaided, are self-motivated and develop the ability to evaluate their own work.

The creative classroom is one in which thinking is valued far more than memory, one in which the child expects to make a contribution that is valued and respected.

The teacher establishes a balance between psychological safety and freedom so that the student will take risks.

This balance allows freedom to think and to be adventurous but not behavioural freedom which leads to chaos.

The teacher is the facilitator, not the only authority with the right answer.

She is the guide, the prompter, the change-agent.

The non-creative classroom by comparison is one in which the teacher is authoritarian, rigid, dominated by time, insensitive to students' emotional needs, unwilling to give of themselves, preoccupied with discipline and the giving of information.

Checklists

Checklists have been widely advocated as a way to improve the efficiency of teacher judgement. Their disadvantage is that they can be rather subjective with no indication of how well a child should score to be considered gifted. However, a good checklist can prove helpful in alerting parents and teachers to the possibility that they may be misjudging some children and will encourage them to look for signs of talent which may have been overlooked. Checklists can also influence strategies and open up a dialogue with children and parents. (See George 2003: 8ff. for other examples of checklists.)

I developed the checklist below in workshops for teachers during a lecture tour of New Zealand and it has proved to be very popular. None of the behaviours in the list should be taken as proof of high ability but they may alert teachers and parents to the need to question the reason for their occurrence. If a child measures up to a number of the attributes listed – and the child in the completed checklist certainly does – then you should enquire further into that student's ability.

Completed checklist

Child's Name: Mary Jones Sex: F Age: 9y 3m DOB: 3.4.93					
Characteristic	Poor	Weak	Average	Good	Exceptional
Use of language					X
Reasoning ability					X
Speed of thought					X
Imagination				X	
Memory					X
Observation				X	
Concentration			X		
Questioning					X
Makes original suggestions				X	
Problem solving					X
Extent of reading					X
Routine work	X				

Checklist: Bright child – gifted learner

Bright child	Gifted learner
Knows the answers	Asks the questions
Is interested	Is highly curious
Has good ideas	Has wild silly ideas
Works hard	Plays around yet tests well
Answers the questions	Discusses in detail, elaborates
Top group	Beyond the group
Listens with interest	Shows strong feelings/opinions
Learns with ease	Already knows
Enjoys peers	Prefers adults
Grasps the meaning	Draws inferences
Completes assignments	Initiates projects
Is receptive	Is intense
Copies accurately	Creates a new design
Enjoys school	Enjoys learning
Absorbs information	Manipulates information
Technician	Inventor
Good memorizer	Good guesser
Enjoys straightforward sequential presentation	Thrives on complexity
Is alert	Is keenly observant
Is pleased with own learning	Is highly self-critical

Experience tells me that you will have a large number of bright children who will be a great pleasure to teach, but fewer gifted learners.

A word about testing

The use of norm-referenced and criterion-referenced baseline tests, in conjunction with national tests, allows you to demonstrate the value-added component that your school has delivered, thereby making any national test results more meaningful. For example, criterion-referenced baseline assessments such as *The Early Years Easy Screen* (Clerehugh et al., 1991) and norm-reference tests such as the *LARR Test of Emergent Literacy* (Downing et al., 1993) could be used to assess children on entrance to primary school.

Tests are not constructed with the intention of students being able to get every question correct, although many able children will. Depending on the difficulty level of a particular test, they may only be required to score 50 per cent to be performing at the established mean or average level for their age. You may also be pleasantly surprised to find that a pupil does better than expected, and often gifted and talented children will enjoy these tests.

One of the major benefits of using a suitable test is that it can provide teachers with objective evidence. It is very easy for us to let our judgements be influenced by our subjective feelings and past experiences, so often there appears to be an expectation gap between how teachers think their pupils will respond to a test and how pupils actually perform. Conversely, another problem is low expectations of their children from some parents. Therefore, it is very important when designing, trialling and standardizing tests to ensure that students feel comfortable with them and are sufficiently motivated to do their best.

As to the choice of test, this is difficult as there are so many available, but the table below shows a variety of well-tried and recommended tests, which are all published by NFER-Nelson. Remember: criterion-reference tests will tell you *what* an individual pupil knows and can do, whereas a norm-reference test will tell you *how* individual pupils are performing in relation to age-related peers. If put to proper use, both kinds of information can greatly benefit pupils by ensuring easier differentiation of work at levels suitable for the individual and providing a measure of the national average performance. In my experience the AH series of tests – starting with AH1 for 5-year-olds and going up to AH6 for A level students – are very helpful. The CAT test is the most popular in the UK, and is used by 80 per cent of secondary schools, normally in Year 7. However, there are other tests such as MidYIS and PIPS which are now widely used. Many teaching colleagues will agree that we over-test in this country, so it is recommended that we also use other criteria in order to build up a profile of the whole child (see 'How to identify gifted and talented children' on pages 38–9).

Formal tests for identifying gifted and talented children

Title	Type	Age range
Cognitive Abilities Test (CAT)*	Verbal, non-verbal and quantitative reasoning	8–15
NFER-Nelson Verbal Reasoning Series	Verbal reasoning	8–13
NFER-Nelson Non-Verbal Reasoning Test Series AH Series*	Non-verbal reasoning Non-verbal, verbal, numerical and perceptual	5–adult 5–adult
Raven's Progressive Matrices and Vocabulary Scales NFER-Nelson Special Access Test Series	Verbal and non-verbal reasoning Verbal and non-verbal reasoning. English and maths	5–adult 11+
NFER-Nelson Item Bank	Verbal and non-verbal reasoning. English and maths	11+

Title	Type	Age range
Richmond Test of Basic Skills (2nd edn)	Vocabulary, language, study skills and maths	8–14
British Picture Vocabulary Scale (BPVS)	Vocabulary	2.5–adult

* Possibly the best test for gifted and talented children.

Academic ability is perhaps the major reason why gifted and talented pupils are initially identified, at least within the school setting, because such talents quickly gain the attention of the classroom teacher. It is usually obvious from test results that a gifted child is performing above average in academic subjects. However, many other characteristics affect the manner in which gifted pupils approach a task or study skills. Gifted is as gifted does. I refer you to the model based on Renzulli's work (see the Must, Should, Could model on page 88) which emphasizes ability, creativity and task commitment. I am more concerned that if a child is not motivated and does not enjoy school, then they will not learn. This is when they stray into the unfortunate world of the young, gifted and bored.

Being a creative thinker

Creativity is an area in which gifted and talented pupils often excel – given the opportunity. However, it is an extremely difficult concept to define and subsequently to measure. Creativity is not necessarily correlated to intelligence and research shows that over an IQ of 105 (just above average) there is no correlation between the two. This does not mean to say that an intelligent child cannot be creative, of course, and vice versa.

When it comes to testing for creativity I recommend the Urban and Jellen Tests (Urban and Jellen, 1996), which are now being used in many schools.

In this assessment, in order to achieve a high degree of cultural fairness, a drawing test of figural stimuli is used (see George (2007) for more details). However, I have devised a much simpler three-step test to indicate if a child has creative ability which is suitable for younger children as well as secondary school students (see below). Notice how it starts with the obvious: simply asking them what they think 'creativity' is.

I have had many wonderful discussions with pupils on the meaning of creativity, and the following are just a few examples from Year 6 children, which will probably astound you:

Creativity is when you do something different to what your teacher expects from you, and you do it well.

It's something you've done that's unique or original.

Is completely new and different.

Is about creating something unexpected, or something expected, in an unexpected way.

It is when you create something very good, in an unusual way – sort of like when a teacher doesn't tell you to do something but you still do it!

Three-step creative thinking assessment tool

1.	To begin with simply ask them what they think the term 'creativity' means. You may well be surprised by their answers ...
2.	Get them to list (in three minutes) as many possible uses for a brick as they can. On other occasions it could be uses for a wire coat hanger or a paperclip. Some bright juniors I worked with once recorded thirty-eight different uses for a paperclip.
3.	Ask them to use their imagination and make something creative using the twelve squares below. Give them five minutes for this.

By asking children to discuss the meaning of creativity first, they are then, hopefully, in a position to produce something creative out of twelve squares (see below). In my experience 92 per cent of children tested confine their drawing to inside the boxes, whereas just 8 per cent think quite differently and make whole pictures and/or think outside the box.

Creativity is very subjective which is why some purists reject the test.

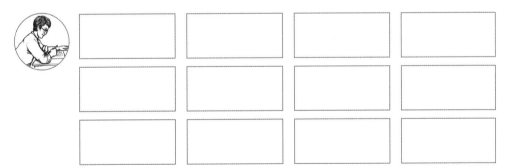

Now show this to a friend and mark each other's work out of 10.

Try to decide which is the most creative, unusual, unique or special using your imagination.

The following are examples of children's responses to this exercise.

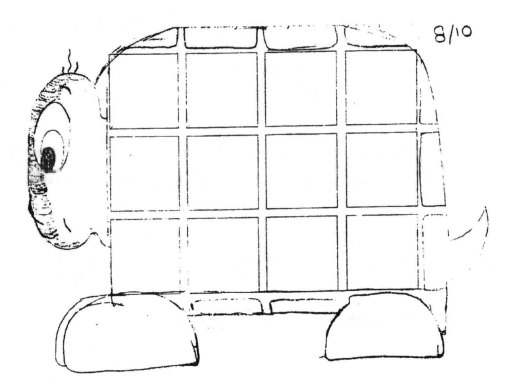

8/10

Now show this to a friend and mark each other's out of 10
Try and decide which is the most creative – unusual

Now show this to a friend and mark each other's out of 10
Try and decide which is the most creative – unusual

Having assessed your students you may like to consider the following questions:

■ Are there major differences between genders?

■ Can the test be applied to children of different countries and cultures?

■ What does the test tell us about children's creative ability?

The work they do and the questions they ask

It is the professional duty of busy teachers to spot talent when they see it. Gifted children are not always consistent in the work they produce, but if they are motivated they can perform exceptionally well. There follows several pieces of work by outstanding children which I suggest indicate an advanced ability (and I am not referring to Key Stage levels!). How would you assess this work?

A topic on dinosaurs by 6-year-old infants. The teacher asked the children how they could solve the problem of cleaning a dinosaur's teeth. This is Daniel's creative solution.

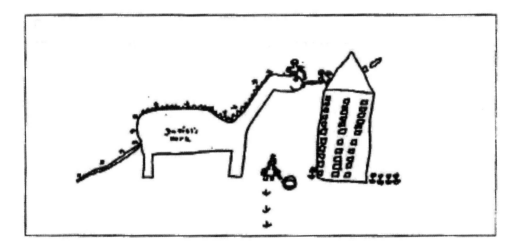

A man climbs the dinosaur's back to its head, where he dangles food in front of its eyes to open its mouth. Another person on the house-roof cleans the dinosaur's teeth with a brush. The person on the ground is putting glue down to keep the dinosaur still. He is wearing a mask because the glue is poisonous.   Daniel

UP IN SPACE.

I am in a space capsule, and I am landing on a big planet with craters in it and it is very cold. I can jump very high and I landed in a crater. There are funny green animals here. There is no one else here except me. I have a space buggy and I drive around space in it. I went on an exploration and found funny flowers with spikes on. They have pink leaves. I was so lonely that I went home.

THE END.

By Karen ·.·. Age 5½

Notice the skills of writing, the language, knowledge, humour and the human touches at the end.

Elizabeth, aged 12, took a different approach from the rest of her class when they were asked to write an essay on conflict.

Conflict surprise (a recipe for war)

Ingredients:	Method:
5 kg of greed	Using a fist, mix in the greed and envy. Let it simmer for an hour. Kick the raw anger in. Squeeze the selfish and add it to thicken the mixture. Sprinkle the mistrust and stir thoroughly. Using a tank (if you have one) firm in the violence. Beat in the misunderstandings. Take a world leader and empty its mind of peaceful thoughts. Using half the mixture refill the mind. Carefully put the world leader back in its place. Using a sword spread the other half of the mixture across one of the world's countries. Remember to stand back after you have done this; you may become a victim of your own creation. Watch for the after-effects. You will enjoy the pain and suffering. You will find it impossible to clean the kitchen when you have finished; all the ingredients will contaminate the rest of the kitchen. Quick tip: for fuller flavour, act first, think later.
2 kg of envy	
1 raw anger	
1 large selfish (very ripe)	
5 g of mistrust	
7 kg of over-ripe violence	
3 large misunderstandings (if you have them)	

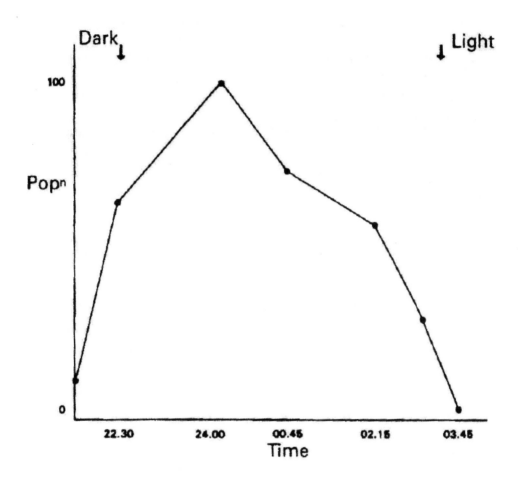

At a Saturday school for gifted children, all of whom had been nominated by their teachers as children who would benefit from being extended, the author did a two-hour workshop based on woodlice. As a result two 9-year-old boys (David and Sean) stayed up all night counting woodlice on a garden wall. This is their result which proves woodlice are strictly nocturnal.

The following are some questions I have been asked recently:

- A 3-year-old asked me on a beach, how does a fly sit down? And as a zoologist I did not know. Indeed, I have been looking at flies ever since, and as yet, I have not seen a fly sit!

- A 6-year-old asked me, if God made the world what did he stand on?

- An 8-year-old asked, why do brown cows eat green grass, and give white milk?

- An 8-year-old asked, if God made the world, why are people so horrible? This question developed into a lengthy discussion about Homo sapiens, which means 'thinking man'. The child said that we do not think. Look at what we are doing to the world.

- A 10-year-old asked me, how do you know when you know? This question, I suggest, is about BA Philosophy level, and you could almost hear Plato posing the problem.

- A 14-year-old boy asked me, why do clouds have edges?

From questions such as these, it is clear that every child is unique and displays his or her giftedness – or in the case of our gifted underachievers, conceals it – in a variety of ways. For this reason it is difficult to define the concept of giftedness or to describe general characteristics according to which a child could be classified in a specific category. It is obvious that a distinction must be made between specific and general giftedness, between intellectual/academic and specific talents, as well as between different kinds of giftedness. It is also understood that we must look at a much wider talent pool and recognize that giftedness is the *potential* for exceptional development of specific abilities as well as the *demonstration* of performance at the upper level of a talent continuum. This is not limited by age, gender, race, socio-economic status or ethnicity.

Unless a child's abilities are known and carefully assessed he or she cannot possibly receive – except quite fortuitously – the programme of work and degree of challenge he or she needs. If our gifted children are to receive social justice within our school system, we owe it to them to identify them and adapt the curriculum to suit their needs and thus prevent any likelihood of them opting out through boredom, frustration or lack of recognition.

No identification strategy is perfect, but to do nothing is an act of choice and is a decision to ignore one section of the pupil population. Yes, criteria must be defensible; but objective criteria should be modified by subjective concern for children. Every child is entitled to the best programme, the most attentive care and the greatest love and respect that we can conceive and provide (see the summary diagram below).

Teachers are reminded that peer group questionnaires, self-evaluation and parent questionnaires are available to build up a holistic model of identification (see George (1997) for questionnaires).

Multiple approach to the identification of the gifted and talented

Tests

Teacher

Parents

Self

Peers

Expectation

Although assessments include creativity tests and checklists, teachers ought to know their children and their abilities and will hopefully take some action to extend their students. We should work in close partnership with parents who should understand their children's aptitudes. We must also ask children what they think they are good at and what they would like to pursue in depth. Finally, the peer group know who are the ablest in the class, who can empathize and who they can go to for advice or crib homework from (ask children to pick a sports team and they can do it very well!).

Teachers are welcome to copy the referral form below which should provide a sufficient summary of a child's abilities. This information can then be given to the GATCO and/or head teacher who hopefully have the authority to make things happen.

Referral form for gifted, talented or underachieving children

I wish to draw your attention to ....

in .... (Class or Tutor Group)

Please find attached the following:

1. Checklist.

2. My written description of the child's classroom performance.

3. Letter from parent and/or parent questionnaire.

4. Test results, including creativity tests.

5. Photocopied evidence from the child's written work.

6. Nomination by self and peer group.

Signed ....

Chapter 3
Provision

Chapter 3
Provision

The education of the child shall be directed to the development of the child's personality, talents and mental and physical abilities to their fullest potential.

United Nations Convention on the Rights of the Child, Article 29

The human mind, overstretched to a new idea, never goes back to its original dimensions.

Oliver Wendell Holmes

Treat people as if they were what they ought to be, and you help them to become what they are capable of being.

Goethe

Think about the teaching practices prevalent in your school and then consider the following questions:

1. Do they properly emphasize the acquisition of a higher order of thinking skills and concepts?

2. Are they flexible and open ended enough for the child to develop at his/her own pace?

3. Is there a learning environment as emotionally protected as it is intellectually stimulating?

4. Do they provide a process that is valuable to the child rather than a product that is prestigious for the school?

5. Are they likely to alienate a child from his/her peer group, and will it be detrimental to the child's subsequent learning – introducing factors that will inevitably be repeated later which could lead to boredom?

Although there are various methods to provide for our gifted and talented children, Ofsted have been critical of many schools in that they seem only to provide more of the same (often death by a thousand worksheets) rather than offering opportunities for children to be challenged to think.

Now consider the list below. To what extent does your school practise these teaching strategies for gifted and talented children?

1. Using the pupils themselves to support other children and also undertake individual advanced studies.

2. Open competition – such as master classes, maths Olympiad, etc.

3. Using the pupil as the teacher – ask children to give a short lesson.

4. Using yourself as a resource – an in-house mentor.

5. Designing a new curriculum – one they would like to pursue in depth.

6. Using the school's facilities better – using children to investigate your inventory.

7. Using teacher's special interests (all teachers have hobbies, interests and talents) and sharing staff expertise.

8. Special school or class responsibilities.

9. Special homework (the best individualized learning there is) – not more of the same.

10. Language classes – perhaps Latin or Chinese.

11. Talent classes – like-minded pupils work together to stretch one another.

12. Specialised training courses – such as university or learned societies, National Association for Gifted Children (NAGC), etc.

13. Extra curriculum provision – such as clubs or societies.

14. Looking further afield:

   a. To local colleges and universities – links with outside expertise.

   b. To specialist organizations – like the Royal Society for the encouragement of Arts, Manufacturers and Commerce (RSA), subject organizations.

   c. To talented parents – Rotarians or other learned individuals.

15. Pupils becoming their own teachers:

   a. Pupils devise the next work card.

   b. Pupils predict the class's next step.

16. Social programmes:

   a. Cooperative work programme.

   b. Sensitivity games – see Circle Time literature.

   c. Building confidence in front of an audience.

   d. Self-critical tasks – marking each other's work makes for better learning.

17. Getting teachers and parents together – running joint evening classes.

18. Observational pairing – ask a good friend to observe a lesson and then revise it.

19. For older students the Open University foundation courses provide excellent enrichment.

20. Acceleration – accelerated learning, moving up the school, partial transfer or withdrawal.

In this chapter I will share with you a variety of strategies that your school can employ to help switch on gifted underachievers. But before I do, a quick word about how to stretch that most important muscle in the fight against gifted underachievement – the brain.

Huge progress has been made over the past decade in understanding how the brain learns. The more we discover the more it becomes clear that there are many myths and misconceptions, so schools and teachers are becoming confused as to what methods and techniques are research based and what is pseudoscience. A full treatment of the current thinking on the brain and learning is beyond the scope of this book but can be found in Ian Gilbert's *Why Do I Need a Teacher When I've Got Google?* (2011) and Andrew Curran's *The Little Book of Big Stuff about the Brain* (2008).

One of the most carefully researched aspects of the learning brain is the impact of enriched and impoverished environments on the brains of animals. It was Charles Darwin who noted in 1874 that the brains of domestic rabbits are smaller than those of the wild variety.

Marian Cleeves Diamond is a leading researcher in this area and her book *Enriching Heredity* (1998) is highly recommended. She suggests that the most important elements when working with children to influence learning and brain growth are:

■ A steady source of positive emotional support.

■ Stimulating all the senses.

■ Providing a nutritious diet with sufficient protein, vitamins and calories.

■ An atmosphere free of undue pressure and stress but with a degree of pleasurable intensity.

■ Presenting a series of novel changes which are neither too hard nor too easy.

■ Promoting the development of a full range of skills and interests that are mental, physical, aesthetic, social and emotional.

■ Encouraging social interaction for a percentage of activities.

■ Encouraging the child to be an active participant rather than a passive observer.

● Learning is mental

● The learner's brain is unique and specialized.

● The brain is situational.

● Unique individuals have different learning styles.

● Learning designs can accommodate individual differences.

● Delivery of learning can respond to personal uniqueness.

● Unique people can be made an integral part of the learning design.

● Learners can be grouped in schools to make the learning more effective.

● Learning through affirmation and discovery can be more effective, fulfilling, enjoyable and longer lasting.

Thinking skills can be strengthened and improved through exercise in a similar way that sports skills can be improved by practice. Creative thinking may be taught directly by helping Pupils to understand imaginative people and processes; critical thinking may be taught by teaching children to observe and look critically at opinions expressed in newspaper articles. A good model is Bloom's Taxonomy (see page 84), and much of the work in the teaching of thinking skills has recognized his impact in this area. His taxonomy describes progressively higher levels of cognitive activity. This encouragement to think is commonly called metacognition (i.e. thinking about thinking) and pupils should be taught to understand their thinking strategies and why and when these approaches may be used.

Young, gifted and stretched – eight great strategies

Skill	Task starter
1. Fluency Quantity of ideas	List all the ... What are all the ...? Write ten ... What are some reasons for ...? How many ...? What are the things ... if ...? Explain how you felt when ...
2. Flexibility Variety of ideas	What are the alternatives to ...? Compare a ... with a ... How are they alike/different? What are the consequences of ...? How many different ways to ...? Give five different reasons for ...

Skill	Task starter
3. Originality New ideas	Plan a … Invent a … Create a … Compose a song about … Think of unusual ways to … Use all of these to make a …
4. Elaboration Adding to ideas	Improve … by … Modify the … so it … Who am I? I lived … Change the … so that … Adapt … Substitute …
5. Curiosity Wondering about ideas	What would happen if …? Where might … occur? Just suppose … What if …? Why do you think …?
6. Complexity Generating alternative ideas	Decide on the reasons for … What are the considerations if …? What questions can be asked to find out about …? What are the consequences of …?

Skill	Task starter
7. Risk taking Exposing ideas to criticism	Rank ... Justify ... Say why ... is the best/worst. Decide ... Give reasons for ... Would you rather be ... or ...?
8. Imagination Thinking beyond the idea	Imagine that ... Think of ... You are a ... (dog/horse/tree). How do you feel about ...? What would it be like if ...? Pretend ...

In summary, we need to:

- Challenge existing ways of doing things as a means of stimulating new ideas.

- Strengthen intellectual abilities through practice and exercise.

- Make decisions which require consideration of the factors involved and possible alternatives.

Perhaps we should be concentrating on 'problem finding' rather than 'problem solving'. Do we ever ask children about the problems in our schools and in our society? For example, what do we do on a wet playtime? How do we prevent litter being dropped in school? Let alone global problems such as the population explosion, pollution or climate change. They often have incredible ideas that we may not even have thought of before.

The question of questions

Often we can stretch children simply by changing our approach to questions. To achieve this, first and foremost, we need to avoid those unproductive questions whereby children only need to *know* rather than to *find out* the answer (see 'Young, gifted and stretched – eight great strategies' on page 68 and 'Thinking skills – some open-ended problems' on page 74).

Instead, here are some alternative questioning strategies to get *all* children's brains going. Teachers are recommended to use the following target sheet which is a helpful tool for tracking children's progress.

 ## Brain-stretching questions

1. **Attention-focusing questions**:
    During initial observation to help children notice details, e.g.
    'Have you seen ...?'
    'What can you hear?'
    'What do you think it is?'

2. **Measuring and counting questions:**
    To move children from qualitative to quantitative observations, e.g.
    'How many ...?'
    'How long ...?'
    'How often ...?'

3. **Comparison questions:**
    To help children order their observations and data, e.g.
    'Which is longer ...?'

'What is the same about these ...?'

'What is different about these ...?'

4. **Action questions:**

   To encourage experimentation and the investigation of relationships, e.g.

   'What happens if ...?' then

   'What do you think will happen if ...?'

5. **Problem-posing questions:**

   To encourage children to set up hypotheses and investigate them, e.g.

   'Can you find the way to ...?'

6. **Reasoning questions:**

   To help children generate hypotheses and explanations for experiences they have had, e.g.

   'Why do you think ...?'

Judicious questioning is nearly the half of knowledge, so quality questioning is a great skill for teachers to learn. Tracking children through school is a difficult problem especially at secondary level. Target-setting is closely linked to identifying learning objectives and focusing closely on the pupils' needs. Targets may be geared towards higher order thinking skills especially for the gifted and talented children and help prevent learning opportunities from being wasted. The table and exercises below can be used to help achieve objectives.

Personal work targets

Name .... Form .... Date		
Area of work	**Student comment**	**Teacher comment**
Performance in the classroom		
Homework		
Tests/examinations		
Aims for future work: 1. 2. 3.		
Agreed targets: 1. 2. 3. 4.		
Review date		
Signed:		
Student		
Teacher		

Thinking skills – some open-ended problems

 Discuss these with a friend and see how many answers/solutions you can find.

Be different, think creatively.

1. You walk into the kitchen and flip the light switch to the 'on' position. Nothing happens. The light doesn't go on. The light bulb doesn't flash and then go off. You don't smell anything burning. What might be wrong?

2. Traffic accidents result in great losses of life and poverty every year. Suppose you were a dictator with absolute power to enforce your demands. What would you do to decrease the number of traffic accidents?

3. There is enough space behind the garage in your back yard for a small garden. There isn't enough room to raise everything you'd like to grow, so you want to plant the things which will grow best. How would you go about deciding what to plant?

4. More and more medical scientists are finding cures for different types of cancer. But it still seems that cancer is killing many more people than it did fifty years ago. Why do you suppose this is so?

5. Think of all the things which have happened in the last one hundred years. Consider the ways people's lives have changed. Suppose you were born one hundred years from now. How would your life be different then than it is now?

Quotations

Here are some profound quotations to make you think. What do you understand from them?

To handle yourself, use your head.
To handle others, use your head.

Anger is only one letter short of danger.

Great minds discuss ideas.
Average minds discuss events.

God gives every bird its food
but he does not throw it into the nest.

Learn from the mistakes of others.
You can't live long enough to make them all yourself.

The tongue weighs practically nothing
but so few people can hold it.

Here are two questions to discuss with your friends (see Ian Gilbert's *The Little Book of Thunks* (2008) for more ideas):

1. Is your brain simply a very advanced computer?

2. Who are you: the thinking student or the questioning student?

Differentiation

Of course, the only true method of providing for gifted and talented children – in a way that benefits everyone – is to differentiate the curriculum properly.

A curriculum which is differentiated for every child will:

■   Build on past achievements.

■   Present challenges to allow for more achievements.

■   Provide opportunity for success.

■   Remove barriers to participation.

This means that teachers should be devising tasks that are appropriate for the range of abilities, aptitudes and interests of their children, and regularly reviewing pupils' progress through observation, discussion and testing. This will lead to variation in the tasks pupils undertake and the need to offer support for individual work, both in person and through the ready availability of appropriate resources.

Differentiation has become a live issue because schools experience difficulty in coping effectively with the wide range of pupils that come through their doors who are chiefly taught in mixed-ability classes. Mixed-ability grouping is often taken for granted; on the whole it is well executed in primary schools but is seen by some as a threat to standards in secondary schools.

Differentiation is not a way of helping slow learners or disaffected pupils. Nor is it just about stretching the clever child. Differentiation is about *all* children because *all* children are different; one of the fascinating aspects about being a teacher is this very fact of human variation. Differentiation, then, is the process by which curriculum objectives, teaching techniques, assessment methods, resources and learning activities cater for the needs of all pupils. *Differentiation means making the whole curriculum accessible to all individuals in ways that meet their learning needs.* This is as good a definition as any and so it has become the lynchpin of the entitlement curriculum, yet it is meaningless if access is not available.

The other important point about differentiation is the emphasis upon the individual, which could prove to be much more helpful than using categories like 'slow learner', 'average' or 'gifted' – although it would be foolish to suggest that these categories are insignificant. We are all marked by individuality: our children think differently, behave differently, learn differently, come from different backgrounds and bring different skills, attitudes and abilities. For this reason, I regard differentiation as an issue affecting *all* pupils of every age and every school in every kind of grouping.

The two main aims of using differentiation in your teaching should be to raise the achievement of all pupils, and to ensure success for all pupils, so that they reach their own personal best performance.

The following diagram illustrates the full range of differentiation strategies.

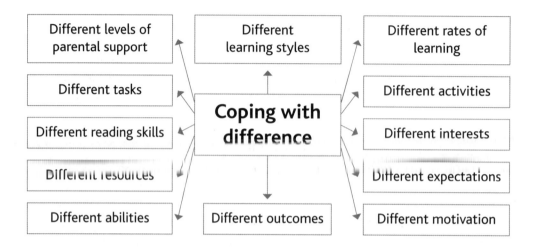

The following exercise provides teachers with an opportunity to arrive at a common understanding of differentiation strategies and their implementation.

Managing differentiation exercise

In your teaching practice, have you considered any or all of the following strategies for improving access to the curriculum for able children or indeed *all* children? Mark on the line where you think you are.

A little   *A lot*

This term (choose any three-week period) I have used the following approaches:

1. Didactic exposition

2. Whole-class teaching

3. Individual work

4. Small group work

5. Partner work

6. Visual material

7. Audio material

8. Role play/simulation

9. Drama

10. Questions at different levels

11. Silent reading

12. Group discussions

13. Survey/questionnaire techniques

14. Practical experiments

15. Work pitched at several levels of response

16. Varied pupil groupings

17. Guest teachers/other adults

18. Differentiated homework

19. Negotiated approaches with pupils directing

20. Contexts outside school (e.g. community, theatre, visits)

21. And add your own.

Points for discussion

Do you have a dominant profile? What do your results show about your teaching style? Discuss these with a friend or peer group. Which strategies are most important for meeting individual needs? Ask a colleague to observe your teaching as a follow-up.

Differentiation is a complex, multi-layered notion related to the ways in which teachers provide for variation in the age, interest, aptitudes and abilities of students. It may be viewed as a rich source of ideas which you can tap into in order to provide learning experiences which meet every individual's needs.

The exercise below may help you and your colleagues to address what differentiation means within your subject area and act as a stimulus to an in-depth consideration of the issues. You will get different results according to the age range taught as well as separate subject areas.

Diamond ten exercise

1. Photocopy the diamond ten sheet.

2. Cut out the ten shapes.

3. Attempt the activity individually.

4. Which diamond would you discard completely as of no value to differentiation?

5. What would be your top three working methods to ensure differentiation?

6. Arrange the diamonds in descending order of priority with your first choice at the top of the shape.

7. Share your conclusions with colleagues.

8. Attempt to arrive at a consensus priority order in your group or department.

I have found that diamond numbers 3, 6 and 10 are the most frequently used methods in schools.

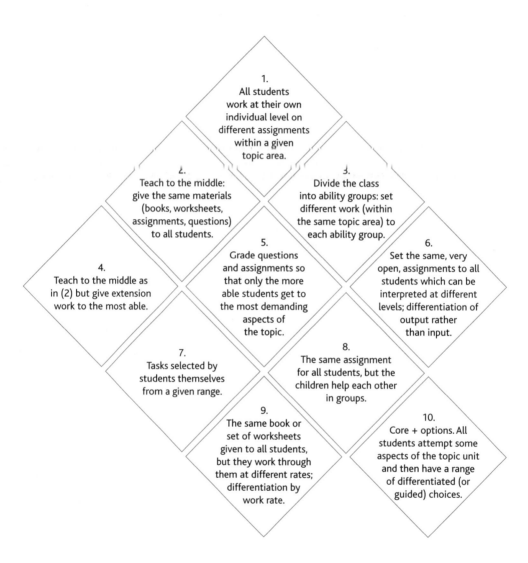

1.
All students work at their own individual level on different assignments within a given topic area.

2.
Teach to the middle: give the same materials (books, worksheets, assignments, questions) to all students.

3.
Divide the class into ability groups: set different work (within the same topic area) to each ability group.

4.
Teach to the middle as in (2) but give extension work to the most able.

5.
Grade questions and assignments so that only the more able students get to the most demanding aspects of the topic.

6.
Set the same, very open, assignments to all students which can be interpreted at different levels; differentiation of output rather than input.

7.
Tasks selected by students themselves from a given range.

8.
The same assignment for all students, but the children help each other in groups.

9.
The same book or set of worksheets given to all students, but they work through them at different rates; differentiation by work rate.

10.
Core + options. All students attempt some aspects of the topic unit and then have a range of differentiated (or guided) choices.

There are many models on the market to support differentiation and some of these are included in the table below.

On page 86 there is an example of a worksheet based on Bloom's Taxonomy and another one on page 140 for early years children. I have used these on numerous occasions with students, with the proviso that 'You do not need to do the whole worksheet, but I trust you to work at the level you feel you are at'. It doesn't take long to check if the child is working at the appropriate level.

Renzulli's Enrichment Triad model has been adapted for the UK as the Must, Should and Could model. There is an example of this in practice in an RE lesson on page 88. The 'must' is the core curriculum, 'should' is the intermediate level and 'could' is for the most advanced students; as you can see from the concept types, they go from simple to complex. This is a very good model for planning differentiation. Edward De Bono's models are well known and the Six Thinking Hats is a good example of this in practice. It is a scaffolding model which can be used for any topic, even for solving the everyday problems that occur in schools. I have known teachers of young children present this model wearing different coloured hats to remind children of the various levels.

Four of the best models of differentiation for teachers

Bloom's Taxonomy	Renzulli's Enrichment Triad
This model assumes that learning proceeds through a number of stages. Activities can be planned to respond to each of the stages, encouraging a broader approach to the topic. *Knowledge:* knowing and remembering *Comprehension:* understanding *Application:* doing, applying what you know *Analysis:* applying what you know *Synthesis:* combining what you know *Evaluation:* judging the outcome N.B. The bottom three levels are especially appropriate for the gifted as they are higher order (divergent) thinking levels.	This enquiry-orientated model incorporates three types of learning strategy, which are used in the order presented: Type 1: *General interest* ■ develop student interest ■ student suggestions/brainstorming ■ community resources, excursions, speakers, films Type 2: *Development of skills* ■ develop thinking skills, e.g. problem solving, group skills ■ process vs. product Type 3: *Investigation of real problems* ■ apply knowledge using enquiry methods – research, interview, analysis

Megarrity's Creative Learning Contracts	De Bono's Six Thinking Hats
Can be based on students' or teachers' interests. Integrates learning activities across subject areas.	This is a scaffolding model which uses parallel thinking to focus on an issue or problem.
Content: What are the major concepts to be studied?	*White hat:* The thinker focuses on the 'pure' facts
Skills: Which learning-to-learn skills are to be practised? Which critical or creative thinking skills are to be included?	*Red hat:* The thinker switches to a 'feeling' mode, uses intuition, senses or emotions without justifying
Learning activities: These are to be completed independently or cooperatively by students, with the minimum of teacher input. Students become responsible for their own learning	*Black hat:* The thinker may ask negative questions or point out errors.
	Yellow hat: The thinker is constructive, considers benefits
	Green hat: The thinker considers creative alternatives
	Blue hat: The thinker monitors thinking and uses this for planning

Open-ended teaching and learning models can be used with all children to build confidence and to individualize the learning experience. The following exercise for pupils on the global warming effect provides examples of progressively more difficult questions and activities.

Exercise based on Bloom's Taxonomy

 Choose one of the following activities at the level you have presently reached in your research. Feel free to devise your own activity if you wish.

1.	**Knowledge/comprehension** What is global warming? How might it affect people? How might it affect the environment? What are the chief contributors to global warming? What does the ozone layer have to do with global warming?
2.	**Application** What can you do in your life to help combat or reduce the effect of global warming?
3.	**Analysis** Compare life with and without global warming. Would it be the same or different? What might people not be able to do in a world severely affected by global warming? How are the consequences of global warming similar to nuclear radiation? How are they different?
4.	**Synthesis** Design a world system in which global warming has been brought under control. How can we work together as a school/community/world to reduce the effect of global warming?

5.	Evaluation
	What obligations do we have to help reduce ozone depletion and global warming?
	Do some people have a bigger obligation than others?
	If so, who and why?
	What do you consider will be the most effective ways of going about reducing global warming?

The Must, Should and Could model is a simpler method of differentiation (see table below for an example from an RE lesson). The key features are:

■ Concepts – the general idea or notion.

■ Knowledge – what is known in an ordered way and can be used.

■ Skills – the ability to perform a task.

A Must, Should and Could plan for a celebration in religious education

	Must	**Should**	**Could**
Concepts	The importance of celebration Identification of our differences/ similarities	Secular/religious celebration	National/cultural implications for government and minority groups
Knowledge	Know the names of Christian, Muslim, Hindu and Jewish festivals Know some ways of celebrating	Stories behind each festival Match up particular customs with its festival	Knowledge of other groups and their festivals
Skills	Listening/ talking following instructions Social skills Empathy	Mapping skills Recall	Questioning synthesis

In pairs put the material you have prepared for another topic into the same framework.

Other aspects of provision for gifted and talented children

Many schools in countries such as New Zealand and Canada have already established good systems for mentoring gifted and talented children, and these practices are now developing rapidly in the UK. The programme pairs individual pupils with an in-house mentor – a sixth former or teacher – who has advanced skills and/or experiences in a particular discipline and can serve as a guide, adviser, counsellor and role model.

Teachers should be humble enough to realize that it is not always possible for them to extend gifted and talented children to the full, but that there are many people in the community who would be delighted to help in various ways. These could be parents, members of the local Rotary Club or business people. In a typical scenario, an adult mentor and a student meet regularly over a period of months, with the student possibly visiting the mentor on a job site to learn first hand the activities, responsibilities, problems and life-style associated with a particular business or profession. Alternatively, and more likely, the mentor will visit the student at the school. Of course, mentoring presumes a commitment on the part of the student and the mentor to plan a detailed sequence of learning activities designed to achieve a specific goal.

This could fit well with career development as this is one of the few areas of provision which is supported by research (Shore, 1991). Career counselling helps children to mark job possibilities early on and should favour open-ended choices that allow for further challenge and growth. This is important for the broadly gifted child who is good at everything and yet, having gained 10 A grades at GCSE, has to make an informed decision about A level courses.

Some parents put considerable pressure on their children to follow in the family business or to enter a career that does not coincide with the child's true interests. Girls in particular may need convincing that career and family are compatible, and children from poor backgrounds and some ethnic groups may need their sights setting higher. Professional role models from similar disadvantaged backgrounds can be a vital component of a successful careers service. Excellent work is being undertaken in Gateshead at present which includes giving children a positive work ethic.

Schools may like to use the following survey to recruit mentors from parents, local businesses, Rotary Clubs and so on.

Community Resource Survey

To Parents and Friends of the School,

We now have a policy in the school for supporting our most able children and we are looking for volunteers to share their knowledge and experience with our children. We are aware that our community is represented by many professions, trades and vocations, as well as hobbies and interests. If you are willing to support us in this way, then we would appreciate it if you would complete this form and return it to the school as soon as possible.

Name

Address

Occupation

Business Tel. No.

Home Tel. No.

Below are areas which could supplement the curriculum for the children and to extend them in order to help them reach their full potential. Please complete the form by indicating what you could offer, e.g. talk, practical demonstrations, written materials, visual aids or displays.

Sciences:

Biology

Conservation

Geology

Chemistry
Astronomy
etc.

Professions/trades:
Doctor
Paramedic
Nursing
Law
Vet
Plumber
Policeman
Engineer
etc.

Hobbies:
Photography
Stamps
Music
Painting
Fishing
Gardening
Model making
Horses
etc.

Social Sciences:
Travel
Geography
History

Economics

Sociology

etc.

General:

Arts, crafts

Music

Literature

Business

Languages

Social Work

Journalism

Insurance

etc.

Acceleration

*'I learned nothing, but I got it
all over in two weeks'*

Any teaching strategy that results in placement beyond the child's chronological age is labelled 'acceleration'. This is the most popular way of coping with more able children and research has supported its use with gifted students (Brody and Benbow, 1987; Shore, 1991).

Acceleration offers students the opportunity to select a programme of work that is both challenging and interesting to them. In many countries this means moving up the school by one or two years. By allowing a gifted child to jump some of the normal school curriculum by moving into an older class, it is hoped that the student will be more stimulated, less bored and enjoy school more. Early entry is also one of the easiest administrative ways out of the problem. Nevertheless, such programmes should always be designed to produce sensible, defensible and valuable educational goals.

In my opinion, the case of Ruth Lawrence, who went to Oxford University at 13 to read mathematics, is a ridiculous case of a child being accelerated many years ahead of her age group.

Early entry is not favoured in the UK where it is believed that children need to be well rounded and mature enough to move on physically and psychologically. We also tend to assume that gifted children will automatically reach high attainment targets. However, there is little cognizance of the wide range of ability found in a classroom of children or of their different needs; the curriculum content is often the same for all.

I believe that acceleration should mean stepping up the learning in the classroom – not simply skipping a year or two. Beneficial solutions include telescoping (or compacting) the curriculum by eliminating tasks that are repetitive, reproductive and regurgitative. This frees up time for different and challenging work, thus improving motivation and preventing laziness and underachievement, and also curbing the arrogance that can develop in some children.

Gifted children should have the opportunity to work at their own rapid pace, to progress through and out of primary school into the secondary phase and beyond. Acceleration speeds up learning time to match a student's potential and capabilities. It should mean doing less and learning more.

What does an acceleration programme entail?
■ Early entry
■ Class hopping
■ Telescoping
■ Subject acceleration
■ In-class acceleration
■ Whole-class acceleration
■ Curriculum compacting

Computer technology

Computer technology is an educational resource which is now exploited widely within our schools and has been fully recognized in the National Curriculum. ICT can engage and excite children as well as enriching their learning. It also offers a good example of the individualization of learning, which evidence from schools shows to be of great benefit to some children who can advance at their own pace and in their own time. There are now numerous useful websites available (please see the Resources section).

Paradigm on instructional strategies

Old paradigm	New paradigm
Teach advanced thinking processes to gifted students (creative problem solving, logical analysis, etc.) with the assumption that they can be applied to various content fields.	Teach students instructional strategies that encourage student independence and enquiry (e.g. problem-based learning) within the framework of specific curriculum content.
Emphasis placed on mastering systems of thinking.	Emphasis on mastery of content standards through enquiry, problem finding, etc.

The effects of technology

Teachers and professors were the gatekeepers of knowledge, controlling students; access to understanding and wisdom.	The internet opens access of information to students who no longer have to be dependent on their teachers.
This powerful position controlled the flow of information and often limited gifted students' growth.	An unsolved problem is how to evaluate valid from invalid information and how to rate sources of information.

Producing a successful school policy for the gifted and talented

A coherent school policy for the gifted and talented should include the school's philosophical approach and the practical mechanisms which will convert policy into practice. The following factors should be included:

1. General rationale:

    - Why such a policy is needed; general empathy but also political advocacy.

    - Where it links into general school aims and philosophy.

    - Helping to raise the standards of all pupils in the school.

    - Rationale for undertaking this work.

2. Aims: what the school aims to provide for gifted and talented pupils:

    - Entitlement to appropriate differentiated education.

    - Work at a high cognitive level.

    - Opportunities to develop specific skills or talents.

    - A concern for the whole child (emotional, social, spiritual, health, intellectual) – the affective curriculum.

3. Definitions in order to cast the net wide – multiple talents:

    - Global research definitions.

4. General overall approach:

    - In-class provision.

- Setting.

- Withdrawal.

- Acceleration.

- Higher order thinking skills.

5. Identification and monitoring schemes:

    - Intelligence and multiple talents.

    - Assessment to avoid underachievement.

    - Tracking.

    - Checklists and creativity tests.

    - Nominations – parents, peers, self.

6. Organizational responses:

    - Acceleration.

    - Working with older pupils.

    - Withdrawal across year groups.

    - Provision for exceptional pupils, e.g. monitoring.

    - Quality of learning and standards achieved.

7. In-class approach (this is crucial):

    - Curriculum provision.

- Enrichment/extension.

- Working with others of like ability.

- Setting and grouping arrangements.

- Differentiation and flexible learning.

- Challenge within subject areas.

- Development of opportunities.

- Differentiated homework.

- Equal opportunities.

8. Out-of-class activities:

   - Enrichment days or residential courses.

   - School clubs.

   - Musical and sporting opportunities.

   - Partnership with parents.

9. Personal, Health and Social Education:

   - The affective curriculum (see Chapter 4).

10. Responsibility for coordinating and monitoring progress:

    - Named GATCO.

    - Named class or subject teacher.

11. Process for review and development:

- Education.

- Teacher assessment.

- Pupil self-assessment.

- Analysis of standards achieved.

- Consultations with pupils and parents.

12. Use of outside agencies for training, provision and qualifications.

13. Governors' involvement:

- Staffing policy.

- Job descriptions.

- Provision of resources.

- Celebration of achievement.

- Governor responsibility.

In conclusion

It is a good idea to conclude the policy with a list of key points which high-light the needs of able pupils (see also the Quality Standards diagram on page 8):

■ The opportunity to work at an increased pace.

■ To operate from their appropriate starting point, not an artificial one to conform to everybody else.

■ To require less practice at tasks, not more.

■ Less detailed instructions.

■ More independence of study.

■ A reduced number of steps in a process.

■ Open-ended situations.

■ Abstract tasks.

■ The need to fail.

■ A wide variety of opportunities.

■ To be treated as a child whatever the intellectual level reached.

■ Contact with teachers and a mentor.

■ Creative opportunities.

■ Programmes for their own benefit, not their parents'.

■ Space to experiment.

■ Appropriate question-and-answer sessions.

■ Contact with peers and/or adults with similar interests and capabilities.

■ The chance to take risks in an organized way.

Much of the above can be summed up by the following four factors:

■ The quality of the teacher's questioning.

■ The quality and complexity of the pupil's activity.

■ The removal of unnecessary repetitive practice.

■ The availability of adequate resources.

Chapter 4

Self-Esteem and the Gifted Underachiever

Chapter 4
Self-Esteem and the Gifted Underachiever

The intuitive mind is a sacred gift, and the rational mind a faithful servant. We have created a society that honors the servant and has forgotten the gift.

Albert Einstein

To be taught is nothing; everything is inside waiting to be awakened.

Paracelsus

Being a gifted or talented learner does not necessarily mean being a motivated learner. Similarly, very able children may be highly motivated in areas that interest them, but poorly motivated in areas prescribed by teachers or parents. For a child that lacks motivation in all areas, self-esteem could well be the key to developing self-confidence and self-motivation. *Feeling* esteemed means sensing approval by someone whose endorsement matters to you, while *experiencing* self-esteem means loving yourself, whether others approve of you or not. If we have high self-esteem we are convinced of our own abilities and feel in control of our lives and of our learning. We are confident of our abilities and have a strong feeling of self-worth.

There is some evidence that gifted and talented pupils often have low self-esteem because they are put down by their peer group (George 1997). What is more, they sometimes feel they cannot do enough for their parents who have such high expectations of them. Therefore, they often feel 'different', have a poor opinion of their abilities and compare themselves unfavourably to their peer group – all of which produces a negative attitude to life and learning.

I think the issue of self-esteem is important in raising achievement and therefore it is important for teachers to understand this concept.

Self-esteem is the disposition to experience oneself positively; being able to cope with the basic challenges of life leads to happiness. This means:

■ Living consciously.

■ Self-acceptance.

■ Self-responsibility.

■ Self-assertiveness.

■ Living purposefully.

■ Personal integrity.

■ Self-love.

Self-love implies care, respect and responsibility for and knowledge of the self. Without loving ourselves, we cannot love others (although we should not confuse self-love with self-centeredness).

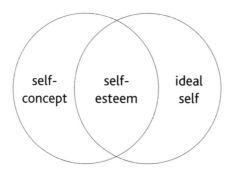

Self-concept means how we feel about ourselves at this moment in time. However, we also have a sense of our ideal self (e.g. where we would like to be in five years time). The closer the self-concept and the ideal self are, the better our self-esteem. This entails knowing ourselves really well, warts and all.

I often give mock interviews for young people who are going for jobs and university places. To help in this process I always recommend the candidates perform a SWOT analysis on themselves beforehand, during which they write down what they consider to be their **S**trengths, **W**eaknesses, **O**pportunities and **T**hreats. This is a very good exercise in building up a truthful portrait of the self.

SWOT analysis

Strengths	Weaknesses
Opportunities	Threats

Of course, much of this chapter applies to teachers and other adults as well as to the children in our care. There are times when all of us feel unappreciated by our head teacher, our parents or even the children we are teaching, so we need to build self-esteem in ourselves and our profession. Excellent teachers need a sense of security and personal competence and a feeling of identity, belonging and purpose.

It is important to consider this issue in greater depth and to include some practical examples.

EQ as well as IQ

Emotional intelligence (EQ) is about being aware of and being able to articulate our feelings. It is about understanding ourselves – how we relate to others and how others perceive us. It helps us to understand something about how other people may be feeling and enables the development of deeper and more fulfilling relationships. It also improves our ability to manage and resolve conflict when it arises. This is essential to collaborative and cooperative learning in the classroom as well as in the workplace.

Not to mention SQ!

It is in the nature of spiritual intelligence (SQ) that it is difficult to define. One point to make clear is that it is quite separate from organized religion. (If you are interested in this area it is worth reading Danah Zohar and Ian Marshall's *SQ: Spiritual Intelligence* (2000)). SQ is about questions more than answers. It lives in stories, poetry, metaphor, uncertainty and paradox. One of the qualities of SQ is wisdom, which includes knowing the limits of your knowledge. In other words, being wise is often about knowing how stupid we are. Other ingredients are values such as courage, integrity, intuition and compassion. But SQ means more is less, rather than less is more, so the process may involve un-learning what others have taught you.

Spirituality is an essential component of a holistic approach to life and work and it finds expression in creativity and all forms of the arts. Antonio Damasio (1994), a neurologist who has studied the links between cognitive and emotional intelligence, believes that spirituality is the 'glue' that holds together our conscious intellect and our intelligent action.

In this age of uncertainty, when changing events and situations appear to be beyond our control, children need to develop their inner strength so they can adapt rather than give up or give in when things get tough. Spirituality sustains us from the inside when all else falls away. We use our SQ to dream, to inspire, to raise ourselves up.

Spirituality checklist

■ Spirituality can be thought of as our personal inner world of thoughts and feelings.

■ Spirituality is what we use to solve problems of meaning and value.

■ Spirituality helps us to place our actions and our lives in a wider and richer context.

■ Spirituality is our compass and it helps us to live life at a deeper level.

■ Spirituality is what joins us with our families, our community, all people and living things, the universe.

■ Spirituality is what we develop when we reflect on ourselves, our ideas and feelings when we are alone.

olistic perspective, we are individuals with a mind, a body and a interconnected and arranged in a pattern that means that the whole is greater than the sum of the parts. We can look at our various types of intelligence in the same way; but increasingly most of our school education is based on cognitive intelligence. We teach children about the sun, the moon and the solar system but still miss the radiance of the sunset.

In our society we have developed the intellect while neglecting our emotions and our spiritual life. If education was more holistic, we would learn to balance our intellect with our emotional and spiritual growth, and as educators we would take responsibility for our personal as well as our professional growth. The words 'health', 'wholeness' and 'holiness' all come from the same root: the Greek word *holism*.

Academic/cognitive intelligence on its own offers little preparation for the emotional challenges we will meet in the course of our lives. EQ represents the factors that can lead you to healthy relationships and the ability to respond to the trials of life in a positive manner. It is about your capacity to manage emotions rather than the other way round. It is also linked to intellectual intelligence because before we can manage our emotions we need to be able to recognize them. Emotions are simply energy (E = motion energy in motion). An emotion without a physical expression is simply a collection of thoughts; talking about our experiences means having a language of feelings. We also need to be able to ask others for help. In my experience the possession of a Y-chromosome seems to be a handicap as girls certainly seem to have better emotional intelligence than boys.

Most educationalists have accepted Howard Gardner's (1983) concept of multiple intelligences, rather than just intelligent cognitivity, although his theory is as yet unproven. I would like to suggest that there are such things as emotional intelligence and spiritual intelligence. IQ does not predict happiness, but EQ and SQ do; but both are extremely difficult to measure which is possibly why Gardner does not include these in his list of eight intelligences.

1. Verbal/linguistic
2. Musical/rhythmic

3. Logical/mathematical

4. Visual/spatial

5. Body/kinaesthetic

6. Interpersonal

7. Intrapersonal

8. Naturalistic

I would like to add practical which the Germans call *technik*.

Many gifted and talented students show great insights in this area of spirituality and ask incredible questions about God and the meaning of life. These children therefore need to be given the space to discuss these matters.

The following poem was given to me recently by an education officer at a conference. It was written by a 13-year-old boy from Lancashire who was very badly behaved, and yet he writes poetry like this. I suggest he understands himself well, and has considerable emotional intelligence.

Outside, Inside

Outside people are scared of me

Inside I don't know why

Outside I think I know what I am doing

Inside I don't have a clue

Outside I am angry

Inside I am kind

Outside I don't know how to spell

Inside I think the words look w(r)ong

Outside I don't try

Inside I want to learn.

Practical strategies to improve self-esteem

Good schools have always included Circle Time or Personal, Social and Health Education (PSHE) into their curriculum during which children are given the opportunity to discuss emotions such as anger, hurt, love and fear – thereby building up self-esteem. There are now excellent courses in which teachers and others are trained to be school counsellors. However, children are not computer hardware onto which software can be installed. They learn emotional intelligence through relationships and natural give and take with friends, neighbours and above all parents, as well as through television and magazines

Schools should aim to develop the following skills in their students:

- Empathy – the ability to understand why and how someone is feeling the way they do.

- Sympathy – the ability to join with others and experience a feeling.

- Consideration – respecting and valuing others.

- Sharing and cooperation – collaboration and negotiation skills.

- Listening and responding appropriately.

- Self-awareness.

- Self-confidence.

- Self-discipline.

- High self-esteem.

Below are a range of successful strategies I have used or developed that will help to raise self-esteem for all students, but are of particular value for gifted underachievers.

9. Class meetings, Circle Time and PSHE – in a circle, pass on a smile or frown, a touch or a handshake. Or ask children to say three things about themselves that someone else would not see by looking at them. Suggest the teacher goes first as this builds confidence enabling children to start disclosing feelings and emotions. (Please ensure that children are allowed to sit out or miss a turn if they are uncomfortable – see Mosley and Murray (1998) for tips and advice on Circle Time.)

10. Drama – drama/role play to express feelings.

11. Video rewind game – used to look at behavioural incidents.

12. Artwork – to express feelings.

13. Dance – body freedom and expression.

14. Music – to explore feelings, rhythms and patterns in pairs, responding to each other.

15. Values education – for instance, at the start of each week (form period or school assembly) introduce a value which becomes the theme for the week (see table below for some examples). Children are praised and given public recognition for displaying this value.

Values for living

Peace	Honesty	Hope
Understanding	Happiness	Appreciation
Patience	Cooperation	Humility
Courage	Caring	Friendship
Trust	Love	Freedom
Thoughtfulness	Quality	Tolerance
Responsibility	Respect	Joy

For more on values education check out *The Little Book of Values* by Independent Thinking Associate and head teacher Julie Duckworth (2009).

It should be clear by now that what I am advocating when it comes to teaching the gifted and talented student is that we aim to teach the whole child, not just their academic side.

A case study – talented teenagers

Research conducted by Mihaly Csikszentmihalyi, Kevin Rathunde and Samuel Whalen (1993), which looked at 200 teenagers (male and female) who were outstandingly talented in maths, music, art, science and athletics, found the following conclusions:

1. Must develop skills that can be recognized, for example, study skills and coordination.

2. Appropriate or supportive personality traits:

    ● Energy for endurance and tenacity.

- Open and responsive to ideas.

3. Productive habits:

    - Limited socializing. Some teenagers overdo this to the detriment of their education

    - Concentration on school is one of the most important aspects of their lives.

    - Time alone with no distractions. This equates with intrapersonal intelligence.

    - No jobs after school. These teenagers were not distracted.

    - Much interaction with parents. Parents being the most important teacher.

    - Limited television viewing.

4. Much family support:

    - Family cohesive and flexible. This was an ideal in the exercise.

    - Parents use good discipline – are intellectual and work hard, set the pace and example, i.e. good role models.

5. Teachers who are good role models:

    - Love of their subject. Students catch enthusiasm from their teachers.

    - Caring and are devoted to their students.

6. Requires rewards and recognitions (see Maslow, 1954). Everyone likes to feel appreciated.

Their conclusion is that schools should offer personal support systems to young people including individual tutorials, mentoring and regular meetings with parents.

Personal support system – how to raise your pupils' self-esteem

 The following excercises provide some simple tools for assessing self-esteem in your learners and are good exercise to raise students' awareness.

■ List the names of people you feel you can talk to in your life right now; people who are on your side and are willing and able to listen carefully and non-judgementally to you.

■ When did you last have an important conversation about things that matter to you with these people in the last week, month or year?

■ When things aren't going your way, do you blame others, yourself or the system?

■ Or do you focus on what you can control and work to improve these things?

■ Can you stop worrying about problems over which you have no control and take responsibility for your own behaviour?

■ Do you understand what assertive behaviour is, and do you recognize if your own patterns are passive, manipulative or aggressive?

- Can you offer support to other friends who may be experiencing emotional difficulties and listen empathetically and non-judgementally to them?

- Are you someone who others feel they can trust and confide in about things that really matter – and not just complaints or gossip.

Please answer all the questions. Put a ring around YES or NO.

Name: .... Age: ....

School: .... Date: ....

1. Is your school work good?	YES NO
2. For girls – do you like being a girl?	YES NO
For boys – do you like being a boy?	YES NO
3. Are you strong and healthy?	YES NO
4. Does someone else always choose what you wear?	YES NO
5. Do your parents think you behave well?	YES NO
6. Do other children like playing with you?	YES NO
7. Are you as clever as other children?	YES NO
8. Does the teacher notice when you work hard?	YES NO
9. Are you very nice looking?	YES NO
10. Does your mum or dad like you to help them?	YES NO

---

11. Are you a good reader?   YES NO

12. Are you good at looking after yourself?   YES NO

13. Do you choose your friends?   YES NO

14. Do you have a best friend?   YES NO

15. Is your teacher pleased with your work?   YES NO

16. Do you need a lot of help?   YES NO

17. Are your parents usually fair?   YES NO

18. Do you often get the blame when it is not your fault?   YES NO

19. Do you find sums hard?   YES NO

20. Do you have nice clothes?   YES NO

21. Do other people decide everything about your life?   YES NO

22. Are you the best looking in your class?   YES NO

23. Are your parents proud of you?   YES NO

24. Do you think that wishing can make nice things happen?   YES NO

25. Would you like to be someone else?   YES NO

Ways to boost self-esteem in your classroom

1. Do 'the morning' bit! The morning is very important: welcome each child with a smile.

2. Notice – use names and identify.

3. Listen – ask questions about thoughts.

4. Create a past – reminisce about …

5. Laugh – share a joke and show you are human. Children revel in humour – and it's good for you!

6. Remember – birthdays and events.

7. Admire – out loud to others.

8. Praise – in writing.

9. Respect – family/history/culture.

10. Share – football teams/pop stars/sweets.

11. Steal – crisps etc. (when in the playground) – they appreciate that!

12. Promote – tell good stories to other staff/children/families.

13. Acknowledge – something that they are better at than you.

14. Recognize – around the school not just in lessons.

15. 'I saw this and thought of you' – give them a cutting from a paper/magazine about their football team etc.

16. Collect – grot (this is why we never have enough space!).

17. Contribute – to everyone's learning.

18. Mark – privately.

19. Find – the invisible child who rarely speaks.

20. Confess – to a private interest.

21. Smile – with your eyes!

The following holistic model emphasises the importance of educating the whole child, the parent child teacher relationship and indicates where students spend their time.

Who are you?

Educating the	CHILD	Children spend
Whole Child	Who am I?	17% of working life in school
Health		33% in bed
Wholeness		50% for the hidden curricular
Holiness		

PARENT   TEACHER

The following are practical examples of ways teachers can help raise their students' self-esteem.

This is a simplified model of Maslow's Hierarchy of Needs for students to use (see Maslow, 1943). The aim is for parents and teachers to help students reach the top of the pyramid.

Maslow's triangle

Few reach their true potential

Classwork

1. Explain in your own words what Maslow's triangle describes.

2. Write down a 'plan of action' to enable you to reach your goal in five years time.

3. What do you think is the most important decision you have made in your life so far? What will be your next important decision?

4. Describe the people/events which could shape your future.

Teachers may like to play Louis Armstrong singing 'What a Wonderful World' while studying the globe. Our aim here is to help students to be in awe and wonder of our planet, to respect it and to care for it.

A wonderful world

If the Earth were only a few feet in diameter, floating just a few feet above a field somewhere, people would come from everywhere to marvel at it. People would walk around it marvelling at its big pools of water, its little pools and the water flowing between the pools. People would marvel at the bumps on it and the holes in it, and they would marvel at the very thin layer of gas surrounding it and the water suspended in the gas. The people would marvel at all the creatures walking around the surface of the ball and at the creatures in the water. The people would declare it precious because it was the only one and they would protect it so that it would not be hurt. The ball would be the greatest wonder known and people would come to behold it, to be healed, to gain knowledge, to know beauty and to wonder how it could be. People would love it and defend it with their lives, because they would somehow know that their lives, their own roundness could be nothing without it. If the Earth were only a few feet in diameter. Space Ship Earth.

Our children are the most precious natural resource in the world. Parents and teachers need to get this across to governments and individual students. They are so incredible that there is nothing they can't do. Shakespeare says it beautifully:

What a piece of work is man! How noble in reason! how infinite in faculty! in form, in moving, how express and admirable! in action how like an angel! in apprehension how like a god! the beauty of the world! the paragon of animals!

Hamlet (Act 2, Scene 2, ll. 25–30)

Chapter 5
Very Young, Already Gifted and Potentially Bored

Chapter 5

Very Young, Already Gifted and Potentially Bored

If children grew up according to early indications we should have nothing but geniuses.

Goethe

Giftedness in the very young can be as worrying and frustrating for adults, parents and teachers as it can be joyful and exciting. Childhood is far too precious a gift to squander but a child's talents should be nurtured from the starting point of the individual. To enable very young children to flourish and develop a lifelong love of reading and writing we must adopt a sympathetic approach based on the child's interests and capabilities, rather than their age as matched to a set of rigid targets.

I am surprised that the government still wants to impose a National Curriculum and test the under 5s, despite documented personal evidence from Scandinavia of the folly of this. In the Nordic countries children do not start school until they are 7 and therefore are emotionally more prepared. In Finland, for example, parents are very much involved in their children's education and good nurseries are provided by the state. It is interesting to note that Finland also has the highest literacy rate in the world. We should value the opportunity to deliver the best educational practice from around the world and see any move to impose a single prescriptive pedagogy as a retrograde step.

We expect our children to be able to read, write, listen and communicate, and as parents and teachers we need to give them the tools with which to acquire these skills. However, if formal education begins too soon children will be put off learning. Where success breeds success, failure breeds failure.

We should expect accountability and high standards from early years professionals. More important than formal assessment is the teacher's ability to identify each student's 'catalyst' or springboard for learning. For most very young children, the medium through which they make sense of the world and become successful future learners is structured play. They learn by using all their senses. Any framework needs to recognize that this is key to a young person's intellectual development.

Appetites for learning develop naturally from an early age. This innate development does not conform to a standard model whereby every child has to achieve the same goal at the same time. Children are born with an instinctive intellectual curiosity which must be fostered. A focus on giftedness during the early years does not mean hot-housing children such that they are force-fed information in advance of their interests. As Smutny, Walker and Meckstroth (1997) observe, pumping children full of information is not the same as encouraging them to develop their own special gifts and abilities. Hot-housing promotes adults' ambitions; gifted education seeks to foster the skills and interests of the children themselves. They are children and it is their right to be childlike first and foremost.

There are few studies looking at the effectiveness of early enrichment for gifted learners. However, one analysis (Fowler et al., 1995) offered early language enrichment training to parents of children aged 3 to 24 months. The researchers found that, whereas 4.8 per cent of children whose parents were university educated could be expected to be gifted, a massive 68 per cent of the children who also received early enrichment were later identified to be gifted. Even more astonishing is the finding that while only 0.001 per cent of children could expect to be gifted when their parents did not complete high school, 31 per cent of those children (many from minority cultures) who received early enrichment training were later defined as gifted.

Not simply prep school!

Early childhood centres, nurseries and the foundation year provide a unique education in themselves, rather than simply being a preparation for serious schooling. They are not just a downward extension of the school system, but are uniquely equipped to cater for young people with a broad range of developmental levels. Many children spend as long as 12,000 hours in child care centres, which is only 500 hours less than they would spend in their thirteen years of primary and secondary schooling combined. This fact alone makes these centres an essential educational setting for many young children. What a responsibility, therefore, to educate as well as to care!

It is crucial that early years professionals have an understanding of child development and educate not just the head but the heart and the hand as well. Without this knowledge a ceiling may be set on expectations of children's abilities, particularly as some may find pre-school and early years education sufficiently challenging while others may already have learned what is on offer, especially those highly gifted children who come from homes where there is a wealth of educational experience.

In my opinion, the key aims of any early childhood curriculum should include the following:

- To develop children's curiosity about the world and enthusiasm for learning.

- To impart basic learning skills to children and conceptual knowledge of the world around them.

- To facilitate the development of higher order thinking and problem-solving skills.

- To give children opportunities to be expressive and creative in many domains.

- To help children establish satisfying and successful social relationships.

■ To develop a healthy self-esteem in each child.

Children's needs

Much research has been undertaken regarding development in the early years. For example, it is generally recognized that by the end of the second year of life an infant has gained two-thirds to three-quarters of all the language they will ever use in conversation for the rest of their life (Brierley, 1978).

Nerve cells in the grey matter of a child at birth (A) and of another at six (B)

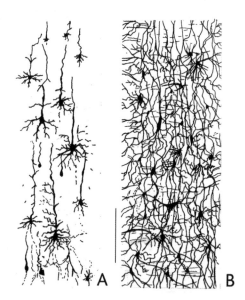

Note: The scale (line) represents 120 µm.

Source: J. Le R. Conel, *The Postnatal Development of the Human Cerebral Cortex*, 8 vols. (Harvard, 1939–1967).

We also know that environmental factors begin to exert an influence on the child before birth and that a favourable pre-birth environment will enhance intellectual growth and development. Every individual is genetically unique and his/her intelligence quotient has a strong inherited base, but intelligence is manifold (as discussed above) and lies beyond narrow IQ tests. Children therefore need individualized learning environments to maximize their potential – something which early years education has long practised.

Factors affecting intelligence

Research suggests that by the age of 5 the brain has reached 90 per cent of its adult capacity and by this time half of intellectual growth is complete. Early nutrition therefore has a crucial effect on the capabilities of the mature brain (Brierley, 1978). Poor diet in pregnancy may not be as important as nutrition in the first two or three years of life because, to an extent, the foetus is protected from inadequate nourishment.

By the end of the first two years of life, the growth spurt of the brain is over. Flexibility of mind and exceptional immaturity at birth compared with other animals give humans a unique capacity for development. Consequently, interaction with a stimulating environment, including language, is crucial to the mind's development.

Learning by doing

The brain is built to mop up language rapidly. Babies are born with a left (language) hemisphere larger than the right. And humans are exceptional in having brain machinery which is able to connect sight, feel and sound patterns. It is essential that from an early age children are talked to and not subjected to 'shut up' answers. Language, like food, is a basic human need.

In respect of learning, large areas of the brain cortex are 'uncommitted' – a blank slate – and need to be filled with good quality experiences. Exploration of the environment is an important biological drive and begins very early. A child learns the nature of things by experience, draws conclusions and then tests them out.

The building up of knowledge through trial and error is the basis for all later intellectual activity. Security, the right amount of intervention by adults and an environment which values explanation and allows it to progress stage by stage will help exploratory learning to flourish.

Experience shapes how our genes are expressed and the major source of experience for children in the early years is other people. What youngsters need is our time, and not necessarily expensive toys.

Effects of exploration

Exploration may feed back to the brain and physically enhance it. Arousing and stimulating interest through exploration increases inventiveness in later life as the brain contains a model of the world built up through senses. A child needs to explore, talk and play with others to refine the model, and this is influenced by the quality of the environment. If deprived of explor-ation, a poor state of mind is created which learns to expect little out of life. Experi-ence shapes how our genes are expressed: 'Train up a child in the way he should go: and when he is old he will not depart from it' (Proverbs 22:6).

Nature or nurture?

Questions about nature and nurture and the interaction between the child's inner and outer world are issues that we should be asking ourselves about as educators. We need to understand how children learn and then give them an environment with a wealth of rich experiences. We also need to be aware of the apparently different learning styles of boys and girls (page 28). It is very important to maintain an integrated curriculum because teaching 'subjects' in the foundation stage could be counter-productive (Porter, 1998). We need to continue to foster natural intellectual curiosity because gifted children are ferocious learners.

The crucial early years and early admission

One of the ways to help the ablest young children is to admit them to school earlier than normal. Studies have consistently been in favour of early entrance (Porter, 1998) although some teachers are still very cautious. It is important that these children are well screened before being admitted because early entry may cause personal as well as academic and social problems. Parents and teachers therefore should work closely together and consider the variables before making this decision. The following points should be considered:

- Reading readiness – This is the most crucial skill for early school success; many gifted children are able to read prior to school entrance.

- Eye/hand coordination – Early admittance children should have reasonable motor skills otherwise there can be unnecessary stress for a young child who is unable to write or draw.

- Health – Children frequently catch common ailments during the early years so a child with a history of good health is more likely to attend school regularly and be more able to concentrate.

■ Social, emotional and physical maturity – This is largely a decision of the parent, in consultation with the teacher, because it is essential that the child is really ready to gain from early admittance. This means the support of a family that values education.

How important is writing?

In slightly older children (5 and 6-year-olds) written achievements are not necessarily the sole criteria for high ability. Many of these students may not have writing skills as advanced as their understanding and thinking abilities; they may not see the point of 'writing it down' and so may not bother. They might find writing to be much slower than their thinking so that they become frustrated, and as a result their writing can be poor. Many gifted young children show their learning achievements as much through what they say as what they write.

Nevertheless, we need to show these students what high quality written work looks like and help them to understand the conventional criteria for judging this work. As teachers, we need to encourage children to deliver to the best of their ability, while also remembering that none of us produces our best quality *all* the time.

Is the child gifted and/or talented?

Many parents are sensitive observers of their own children, know when they have special talents and can inform teachers about their unique abilities. Of course some parents are overzealous and push their children too much even to the extent of home coaching. I give many courses to parents to emphasize this issue and discuss a parent's role in partnership with teachers.

Teachers and parents should watch out for the following qualities which may indicate that a young child is potentially gifted:

1. Shows outstanding ability in manipulative skills and hand/eye coordination.

2. Reaches infant milestones early.

3. Very imaginative in play with good concentration.

4. Makes connections in independent learning and shows initiative.

5. Reads naturally and shows early understanding of the printed word with advanced language skills.

6. Enjoys the company of older children where the language is possibly upgraded.

7. Can categorize, classify and think logically.

8. Is an avid collector and inventor.

9. Has an excellent memory and can recall and relate events in sequence – possibly has a highly developed sense of humour.

10. A natural leader, confident and socially adept.

11. Can be aggressive and attention seeking.

An honest discussion of these characteristics could help in identifying gifted and talented children and assist parents and teachers in coming to a decision concerning early admission to school. However, remember that lists are not prescriptive and not all points will apply to all children.

Joan Freeman (1991) who has undertaken the only thorough longitudinal research on children in the UK, found that for every identified gifted and talented child, there is likely to be at least one non-identified child of comparable ability in that class. Identification is not and cannot be an exact science; therefore it is wrong to heap advantages on the beneficiaries of chance. Nevertheless, these children do have a special need and should be recognized and provided for.

The following list should help focus your mind, as well as that of your colleagues, when it comes to why early identification of gifted and talented children is crucial:

1. It is important to focus on creativity.

2. Gifted and talented children do unusual things.

3. The stakes are high in social and academic development at this early stage.

4. The brain's connections are at their most malleable.

5. It is just as easy to turn children off learning as on.

6. The natural drive is for broad rather than tunnelled experiences.

7. If the capacity to relate to peers and adults is curtailed there are long-term implications.

8. Long-term social and emotional literacy is all important.

9. Early years is at the sharp end of personalization and the system should bend to the individual.

10. There is a danger of too much individualization – sometimes children need to be part of a group in a collaborative and equitable way.

Bearing all these factors in mind, what then can the concerned early years professional do to make sure they are bringing the best out of the very young and gifted child? Here, based on my own experience, is a useful 'to do' list:

1. Listen to the child and talk to him/her sensibly and sensitively.

2. Help the child research for him/herself.

3. Provide interesting and stimulating play equipment.

4. Help the child overcome frustration.

5. Foster social behaviour.

6. Help the child accept that perfection is not always attainable.

7. Encourage the child to meet challenges – he/she can often go further, faster and deeper than we anticipate.

8. Help the child to come to terms with realistic solutions to problems.

9. Work in partnership with parents, who are the most important teachers a child ever has.

10. Encourage the child to read as widely as possible. It is common practice to have boxes of books for children to choose from, but it is also worth encouraging an able child to read aloud to other members of the class.

11. Introduce children to ICT early on as computer skills offer great potential for individualizing the curriculum.

12. Use a network of support both within and outside of school (e.g. National Association for Gifted Children (NACG) and National Association for Able Children in Education (NACE)).

13. Extend and enrich the curriculum through differentiation.

14. Teach higher order thinking skills.

15. Use Circle Time in order to build up emotional and spiritual intelligence.

And, if that wasn't enough, here are a range of other strategies and suggestions you could try to extend the very young and able, which can also be shared with parents:

1. Provide materials that develop the imagination, such as open-ended stories or drawings.

2. Provide materials that enrich imagery – such as fairy tales, folk stories, myths, fables and nature books.

3. Permit time for thinking and daydreaming – just because a child doesn't look like he/she is busy, doesn't mean that the mind is not.

4. Encourage children to record their ideas in binders or notebooks – even playing 'secretary' with the child by having him/her dictate stories to you can be a special way of showing that their ideas are valuable and that you care about what they are thinking.

5. Accept and use the tendency to take a different look – there are many things one can learn about the world by standing on one's head!

6. Prize rather than punish true individuality – it is always possible to find small details about a child's work or behaviour that might make him/her feel as though you have noticed them as a special person.

7. Be cautious in editing children's work – sometimes a word corrected in the wrong place or too many times can stifle a child's creative energy and feeling of worth as a creator.

8. Encourage children to play with words – even in everyday settings such as a car ride or shopping trip, word games like rhyming, opposites and puns can be used to their full advantage.

9. Listen – give undivided attention to perceptions, questions and concerns.

10. Provide a variety of experiences – take trips, visit museums, read books, listen to music, meet interesting people, discuss the chemistry that makes a cake rise, etc.

11. Support and guide a child's own interests.

12. Create an atmosphere where risk taking is OK, even expected.

Practical suggestions

This exercise is designed for Bloom's six levels of activity thus allowing any child to a find task at their own level. It also enables teachers to recognize the thinking level at which individual students are working.

Bloom's Taxonomy based on a food topic for able infants

1. Knowledge:
Name the four main food groups.
Cut out pictures of fruits and vegetables from a magazine.
Label them and name your favourite.

2. Comprehension:
Compare two green vegetables according to their shape, size, taste and how they grow.
Cut out pictures from magazines, or draw them, to make a breakfast, lunch and dinner.
Find out how many calories these foods contain.

3. Application:
Make a collage of foods you like to eat.
Sow a large vegetable seed, watch it grow and draw the stages of its growth.

4. Analysis:
List all the things a cow gives us.
Make up a crossword puzzle of tasty fruits. Give good clues.

5. Synthesis:
Pretend you are a bean seed. Write a story about how you feel as you grow.
Make up your own recipe for a really nutritious cake.

6. Evaluate:
Work out how nutritional your dinner was last night.
'An apple a day keeps the doctor away'. What does this saying mean?
Don't eat between meals. Is this a good idea or not?

Consider the questions the following poem raises – there is much to discuss here.

Why?

Why is grass always green?
What holds up the sky?
Why is hair upon my head?
Why, oh why, oh why?

Why does rain go down, not up?
Why is salt in every sea?
Why is there a sun and moon?
Why is there only one me?

Why do bees buzz and birds sing?
Why do nails grow on my toes?
How long is a piece of string?
Why is it no one knows?

Why is night so full of dreams?
Why do we have one nose, two eyes?
Why do questions never end?
Why are there so many whys?

Robert Fisher

Chapter 6

A Few Words on Parenting the Young, Gifted and Bored

Chapter 6

A Few Words on Parenting the Young, Gifted and Bored

We should encourage a sense of achievement in gifted and talented children in order to help them reach their considerable potential. We do this by building self-esteem, liberating their excellence and turning potential into performance.

The parent–child–teacher partnership

We hear a great deal of rhetoric about the parent–child–teacher relationship alongside the words 'community', 'inclusion', 'stakeholders' and 'partnership'. Involving parents in schools is essential if we are going to turn out well-rounded, happy and fulfilled young people. This is more crucial than ever before because of the rapidly changing world in which we live, where trust in institutions such as parliament, the judicial system, the church and the monarchy are in doubt, as well as the threats posed by climate change, the rising population, shrinking job market, spending cuts and so on. The population is ageing and we are all living longer, so children born today may well live to be 100. The implications of this are enormous.

Newspapers tell us that in the UK we are heading towards 50 per cent of the workforce being employed as information managers or mind workers. In this new world we cannot be educated between the ages of 0 and 20 for the work we will undertake over the rest of our lives.

Teachers and parents should act as good role models who reflect the goals we set for our children. This means interacting with them much more. Children watch us and listen to our every word. If we want them to read, we must read; if we want them to work hard, then we must work hard; if we want them to practise scholarly pursuits, then we must practise scholarly pursuits; if we do not want them to sit in front of the television every evening, then we must not sit in front of the television ourselves.

In spite of the fact that teachers are stressed and over-worked, not involving parents in students' education is not an option. As learning is about the whole of life, teachers must draw on the outside world – including children's families. As Julian Stern (2004) puts it: 'Parents are not cheap substitutes for teachers; teachers are, at best, quite expensive substitutes for parents'.

In most school handbooks, it states that the school looks forward to working in close partnership and harmony with parents to provide the best possible learning environment for their child to develop and realize their educational potential.

If we agree that parenting is the greatest vocation in the world, then we also have to realize the tremendous pressure on parents today.

Parental pressures

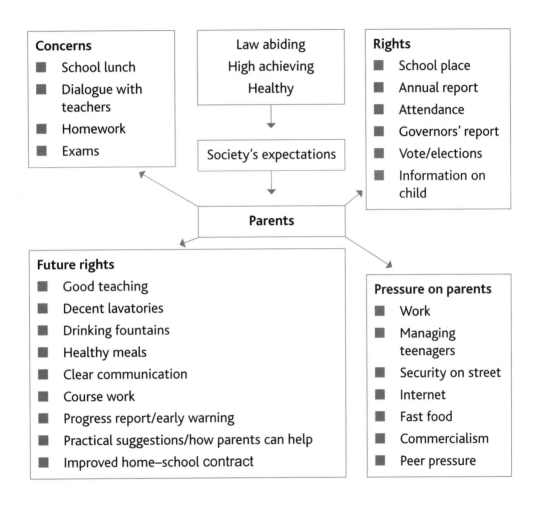

It is not just children but parents who are cracking under the weight of exams, uncertainty about homework and worries about what their child is eating for school lunch – and they often hit a brick wall when they try to enter into productive dialogue with their children's teachers. It is interesting to note the 'rights' of parents in the diagram above – but rights cut two ways. Parents are expected to turn out law abiding, high achieving and healthy citizens while also managing the pressures of work and, in particular, the burgeoning independence of teenagers in a society which seems more full of risks than ever before.

Apart from the right for their children to good teaching, drinking fountains, healthy meals and decent lavatories, what most parents want from a school is a guarantee of clear systems of communication, information about what their children will be learning, progress reports, support when their children fall behind and practical suggestions on how school can help parents.

The partnership in and out of school

In 2007 the DCSF (now DOE) indicated that the progression of gifted and talented students is enhanced by home–school partnerships, that there should be strategies to engage and to reach parents/carers and, in addition, they should be actively engaged in extending provision and be involved in the identification process. Therefore, good communication is essential. Guidelines which were widely accepted and which I continue to suport.

Gifted and talented coordinators also have a role in supporting parents but it is worth reminding parents that their children are only in school for thirty-nine weeks of the year. On my calculations they are in school for just 17 per cent of their waking life; 33 per cent of their life is spent in bed, leaving 50 per cent for the 'hidden curriculum'. School does not finish at 3.30 p.m. and education does not stop at the school gates.

With these statistics in mind, it is clear that children do have time for quality homework; but work that is different from what they have been doing in school all day; work that challenges and excites them to *want* to learn. In the classroom and at home there is no point in giving children twenty exercises to do when they have understood the concept in exercise one or indeed understood the concept before the teacher even introduced it. This is a sure fire route to boredom. There is ample evidence that many children know a lot more than we think they know – and they learn fast. Gifted and talented children should do less and learn more.

The science writer and former Cambridge behavioural scientist Paul Martin states in his excellent book *Making People Happy* (2005) that there are four categories of parent:

- Authoritative parents – love their children unconditionally and accept them for who they are. They keep a close eye on their children, provide them with plenty of support, set firm boundaries and grant considerable freedom within those boundaries.

- Authoritarian parents – in contrast to authoritative parents have a colder parenting style which is more demanding but less responsive to the child's real needs. Authoritarian parents are highly controlling, but are not very warm or loving. They intervene frequently, issuing commands, criticisms and occasional praise, but do this in an inconsistent way.

- Indulgent parents – are responsive but undemanding and permissive. They are warm and loving but set few clear boundaries. They often respond to their children's wishes, even when these are unreasonable or inappropriate.

- Uninvolved parents – are unresponsive, undemanding, permissive and set few clear boundaries, largely because they don't really care very much. Unlike authoritative parents they are neither warm nor firm and they do not monitor their children.

The children of authoritative parents are happier, academically more successful, emotionally better adjusted and have better personal relationships than young people from the other three categories. They adapt better to school or university and perform better in both. What is also interesting is that studies have found that these children are less likely to smoke, take illicit drugs or abuse alcohol. Many psychologists now agree that emotional intelligence is more important than any other type of intelligence and that horitative parenting promotes many of the personal characteristics that typify happy people (see Martin, 2005). These include emotional skills, social skills, freedom from excessive anxiety, a sense of control, self-esteem, resilience, optimism and freedom from excessive materialism.

Our society has made two promises to its children: (1) to prepare a world which accepts them and provides them with the opportunities to live, grow and create in safety, and (2) to help them develop their whole beings to the fullest in every respect. Education is the vehicle through which we try to keep these promises, in partnership with parents. To this end I have compiled a list of ways that parents can keep to their end of the bargain when it comes to bringing the best out of their gifted child.

1. Meet children's needs for love and control, attention and discipline, parental involvement and training in self-dependence and responsibility.

2. Help gifted children to face feelings of difference arising from their exceptional abilities. These reactions might otherwise create emotional problems, disruptive behaviours or withdrawal from a frustrating situation.

3. Present consonant parental value systems.

4. Become involved in early task demands, such as training children to count, tell the time, use correct vocabulary and pronunciation, locate themselves and get around their neighbourhood, do errands and be responsible.

5. Emphasize early verbal expression – reading, discussing ideas, poetry and music.

6. Read to children and have the whole family read together.

7. Emphasize doing well in school.

8. Encourage children to play with words through word games, rhyming, opposites and puns.

9. Provide a variety of books, magazines, puzzles and other aids to home learning, such as encyclopaedias, charts, collections, websites and games to promote the use of the imagination, logical thinking, the drawing of inferences and the making of predications.

10. Help the gifted and talented to become critical viewers and readers by discussing the mass media and literature.

11. Avoid disruption of family life through divorce or separation, and maintain a happy, healthy home (as much as possible!).

12. Because able children often have an awareness of adult problems such as sex, death, sickness, financial difficulties and war, which their lack of experience makes them unable to understand, offer reassurance in these areas.

13. Encourage children to play an active role in family decisions. Listen to their suggestions and apply them whenever possible. For example, when planning a trip or vacation have them participate in decisions about places, routes, food and activities, and assign important tasks appropriate to their abilities (e.g. map reader on a trip or book keeper of the family budget).

14. Explore ways of finding and solving problems by asking questions, posing hypotheses, discussing alternative solutions and evaluating those alternatives. Personal and family situations may be used as well as the larger social issues of the town, the country or the world.

15. Help children to relate to friends who may not be so able. Although gifted children should recognize their abilities, they should also learn to put them into perspective. They should look for strengths in friends as well as for ways to share their abilities productively.

16. Take children to museums, art galleries, educational institutions and other historical places where background learning may be enhanced.

17. Be especially careful not to 'shut up' the child who asks questions. In particular, do not scold for asking or imply that this is an improper or forbidden subject. You may, however, insist that questions not be asked at inappropriate times or require the child to rephrase a question so as to clarify it. Sometimes questions should not be answered completely but the reply posed as a question that sends the child into some larger direction. If you cannot answer the question, direct the child to a resource that can.

18. Avoid pushing a child into reading, 'exhibiting' him/her before others or courting undue publicity. On the other hand, seek in every way to stimulate and widen the child's mind through suitable experiences in books, recreation, travel and the arts.

19. Prize and praise efforts and accomplishments. Support children when they succeed as well as when they don't. Create an atmosphere where risk taking is alright.

20. Encourage children to challenge themselves. Because of their superior abilities, the gifted and talented often work at only partial capacity and still succeed. This approach to learning, however, may ultimately create difficulties because individuals may acquire extremely poor learning habits which they may not be able to overcome when they are sufficiently challenged.

21. Support the school as much as you can by showing an appreciation of busy teachers. Join the Parent Teacher Association. Education is a crucial partnership between parent, teacher and child; teachers cannot do everything.

Both parenting and teaching are great vocations, and our children are the most precious resources in the world. Let us work together to make them whole.

Resources

http://nationalstrategies.standards.dcsf.gov.uk/giftedandtalented

The Department for Education website for teachers and parents which includes events and courses.

www.ofsted.gov.uk/publications

The Ofsted website contains information from Ofsted's research and inspections, including consultations, reports and statistics.

www.londongt.org

The London Gifted and Talented website provides useful information, worksheets, policies and courses.

www.realproject.org.uk

The Realising Equality and Achievement for Learners (REAL) website provides information, worksheets, policies and courses.

www.nace.co.uk

The National Association for Able Children in Education (NACE) has been ably working to support teachers of gifted and talented pupils for over twenty years and has some excellent publications.

www.nagcbritain.org.uk

The National Association for Gifted Children (NAGC) is an excellent organization which was set up to support parents and their children. They also have a helpline for parents on 0845 450 0295.

www.youthmusic.org.uk/musicispower/index.html

A charity which funds and supports music activities for disadvantaged children and young people.

www.youthsporttrust.org

The Youth Sport Trust nurtures young people talented in PE and sport.

www.info4local.gov.uk/subjects/education-and-skills

Provides links to information from across central government on education, educational policy, learning and teaching methods, skills and competences, and special educational needs.

www.creativegeneration.co.uk/guidance.aspx

Gives guidance to teachers in recognizing and inspiring talent in the arts.

www.creative-partnerships.com

The Arts Council provide well funded and successful creativity programmes.

www.bbc.co.uk/schools/bitesize

A great site for pupils to learn how to learn, revise for exams or look for help on subjects and topics.

www.world-challenge.co.uk

Provides educational expeditions to the developing world and closer to home, which teach life skills, stretch comfort zones and expand minds outside the classroom.

www.teachingexpertise.com/gifted-talented

Provides resources and publications on teaching gifted and talented students.

www.thinkersineducation.com/education.html

Provides training and resources on teaching gifted and talented students.

www.english-heritage.org.uk/education

Provides excellent site visits and educational resources.

www.nrich.maths.org.uk

Provides excellent materials to enrich the mathematics curriculum.

www.brookes.ac.uk/schools/education/rescon/cpdgifted/home.html

An Oxford Brookes University resource for those involved in the education of able, gifted and talented learners.

www.worldclassarena.org

An international initiative designed to identify and assess gifted and talented students around the world.

http://world-gifted.org

The World Council for Gifted and Talented Children is a worldwide non-profit organization whose goal is to provide advocacy and support for gifted children.

http://p4c.com

A resource and collaboration service for Philosophy for Children.

www.ingenious.org.uk

A content-rich site bringing together images and viewpoints to create insights into science and culture.

http://ancientolympics.arts.kuleuven.be

The fascinating history of the Olympic Games.

Bibliography

Adey, P. and Shayer, M. (1994) *Really Raising Standards*. Routledge.

Bastiani, J. (ed.) (1997) *Home–School Work in Multicultural Settings*. David Fulton.

Beyer, R. (2008) *Able, Gifted and Talented for the Informed Beginning Teacher*. NACE.

Blagg, N., Bellinger, M. and Gardner, R. (1998) *The Somerset Thinking Skills Course*. Nigel Blagg Associates.

Bloom, B., Englehart, M. D., Furst, E. J., Hill, W. H. and Krathwohl, D. (1956) *The Taxonomy of Educational Objectives, The Classification of Educational Goals, Handbook I: Cognitive Domain*. Susan Fauer Company.

Brierley, J. K. (1978) *Growing and Learning*. Ward Lock.

Brody, L. E. and Benbow, C. P. (1987) Acceleration strategies: How effective are they for the gifted? *Gifted Child Quarterly*, 31: 105 – 110.

Butler-Por, N. (1987) *Underachievers in School*. Wiley.

Buzan, A. (2001) *Head Strong: How to Get Physically and Mentally Fit*. Thorson.

Carter, R. (1998) *Mapping the Mind*. Phoenix.

Clark, C. and Shaw, B. (1998) *Educating Students with High Ability*. UNESCO.

Claxton, G. (2008) *What is the Point of School?* OneWorld.

Cleeves Diamond, M. (1998) *Enriching Heredity*. Free Press/Simon & Schuster.

Cleeves Diamond, M. (1998) *Magic Trees of the Mind: How to Nurture Your Child's Intelligence*. E. P. Dutton & Co.

Clerehugh, J. (1991) *Early Years Easy Screen*. NFER Nelson.

Colangelo, W. L. and Davis, D. A. (1991) *Handbook of Gifted Education*. Allyn & Bacon.

Curran, A. (2008) *The Little Book of Big Stuff about the Brain*. Crown House Publishing.

Csikszentmihalyi, M., Rathunde, K. and Whalen, S. (1993) *Talented Teenagers: The Routes of Success and Failure*. Cambridge University Press.

Damasio, A. (1994) *Descartes: Emotion, Reason, and the Human Brain, Error* G. P. Putnam's Sons.

Dennison, P. and Dennison, G. (1994) *Brain Gym: Teacher's Edition Revised*. Edu-Kinaesthetics.

De Bono, E. (2009) *Six Thinking Hats*. Penguin.

DCSF (2007) *Gifted and Talented Education: Guidance on Addressing Underachievement – Planning a Whole-School Approach*. Department for Children, Schools and Families.

DCSF (2008) *Gifted and Talented Education: Helping to Find and Support Children with Dual or Multiple Exceptionalities*. Department for Children, Schools and Families.

Downing, J., Schaefer, B., Burgess, M. A. and Ayres, D. (1993) *LARR Test of Emergent Literacy*. NFER-Nelson.

Dracup, T. (2009). Speech on DCSF guidelines at the 18th World Conference on Gifted and Talented Children (WCGTC) in Vancouver, BC, 3 – 7 August.

Dryden, G. and Vos, J. (1994). *The Learning Revolution*. Accelerated Learning Systems.

Duckworth, J. (2009) *The Little Book of Values: Educating Children to Become Thinking, Responsible and Caring Citizens*. Crown House Publishing.

Dweck, C. (2006) *Mind Set: The New Psychology of Success*. Random House.

Edwards, B. (1993) *Drawing on the Right Side of the Brain*. HarperCollins.

Eyre, D. (1997) *Able Children in Ordinary Schools*. Fulton.

Eyre, D. (2002) *Curriculum Provision for Gifted and Talented Secondary School Pupils*. NACE/Fulton.

Eyre, D. and McClure, L. (eds) (2002) *Curriculum Provision for the Gifted and Talented in the Primary School*. NACE/Fulton.

Ferretti, J. (2008) *Meeting the Needs of Your Most Able Pupils: Geography*. David Fulton.

Fisher, R. (1997) *Poems for Thinking*. Nash Pollock.

Fisher, R. (1999) *First Stories for Thinking*. Nash Pollock.

Fisher, R. (2000) *First Poems for Thinking*. Nash Pollock.

Fisher, R. (2008) *Teaching Thinking: Philosophical Enquiry in the Classroom*. Continuum.

Fogarty, R. (1997) *Brain Compatible Classrooms*. Skylight Training and Publishing.

Fowler, W., Ogston, K., Roberts-Fiati, G. and Swenson, A. (1995) Patterns of giftedness and high competence in high school students enriched during infancy: Variation across educational and racial/ethnic backgrounds. *Gifted and Talented International* 10(1): 31–36.

Freeman, J. (1991) *Gifted Children Growing Up*. Cassell.

Fullen, D. (2010) *Motion Leadership*. Corwin Press.

Gaarder, J. (1996) *Sophie's World*. Phoenix.

Gardner, H. (1983) *Frames of Mind: The Theory of Multiple Intelligences*. Basic Books.

George, D. (1997) *The Challenge of the Able Child* (2nd edn). Fulton.

George, D. (2001) *Enrichment Activities for More Able Students*. Chalkface.

George, D. (2003) *Gifted Education* (2nd edn). NACE/Fulton.

George, D. (2007) *Making the Most of Your Abilities*. NAGC.

Gilbert, I. (2002) *Essential Motivation in the Classroom*. Routledge Falmer.

Gilbert, I. (2008) *The Little Book of Thunks*. Crown House Publishing.

Gilbert, I. (2011) *Why Do I Need a Teacher When I've Got Google?* Routledge/Farmer.

Goleman, D. (1995) *Emotional Intelligence*. Bloomsbury.

Greenfield, S. (1997) *The Human Brain*. Phoenix.

Gregory, F. and Cox, R. (2009) *Able, Gifted and Talented Learning in English*. Tribal.

Handy, C. (1999) *The Hungry Spirit*. Hutchinson.

Hart, S., Dixon, A., Drummond, M. J. and McIntyre, D. (2004) *Learning without Limits*. Open University Press.

Hoffman, E. and Bartkowicz, Z. (1999) *The Learning Adventure: Learning Skills Workbook for Children and Young People. Learn to Learn.*

Hopkins, D. (2007) *Every School a Great School*. Oxford University Press.

Hymer, B., Whitehead, J. and Huxtable, M. (2008) *Gifts, Talents and Education: A Living Theory Approach*. Wiley-Blackwell.

Ingram, G. (2007) *Meeting the Needs of Your Most Able Pupils: Modern Foreign Languages*. David Fulton.

Jackson, N. (2009) *The Little Book of Music for the Classroom*. Crown House Publishing.

Kennard, R. (2001) *Teaching Mathematically Able Children*. NACE.

Kite, A. (2000) *Guide to Better Thinking: Positive, Critical, Creative*. NFER-Nelson.

Jones, J. (2009) *The Magic Weaving Business: Finding the Heart of Learning and Teaching*. Leannta.

Law, S. (2000) *The Philosophy Files*. Dolphin.

Leat, D. (1998) *Thinking through Geography*. Chris Kington Publishing.

Levy, N. (1994) *100 Intriguing Questions for Kids*. N. L. Associates.

Leyden, S. (1998) *Supporting the Child of Exceptional Ability at Home and at School*. NACE/Fulton.

Lipman, M. (1998) *Philosophy for Schools*. Temple University Press.

Macintyre, C. (2008) *Gifted Children 4–11: Understanding and Supporting their Development*. David Fulton.

McNeil, F. (1999) *Brain Research and Learning: An Introduction*. SIN Research Matters No. 10. Institute of Education.

Martin, P. (2005) *Making People Happy: The Nature of Happiness and its Origins in Childhood*. Fourth Estate.

Maslow, A. H. (1943) A theory of human motivation. *Psychological Review* 50(4): 370–396.

Montgomery, D. (2009) *Able, Gifted and Talented Underachievers* (2nd edn). Wiley-Blackwell.

Mordecai, S. (2008) *Able, Gifted and Talented for the Informed School Governor*. NACE.

Mosley, J. and Murray, P. (1998) *Quality Circle Time in the Primary Classroom*. LDA.

Nailer, S. and Keogh, B. (2000) *Concept Cartoons in Science*. Millgate.

Pohl, M. (2000) *Learning to Think, Thinking to Learn*. Hawker Brownlow Education.

Porter, L. (1998) *Gifted Young Children: Meeting their Needs*. Open University Press.

Renzulli, J. (1977) *The Enrichment Triad Model*. Creative Learning Press.

Sammons, P., Hillman, J. and Mortimore, P. (1995) *Key Characteristics of Effective Schools*. Institute of Education/Ofsted.

Senior, J. (2008) *The Primary G&T Handbook*. Optimus Education.

Shore, B. M. (1991) Building a solid professional knowledge base in gifted education. *Exceptionality Education Canada* 1: 85–102.

Simister, J. (2007) *How To Teach Thinking and Learning Skills: A Practical Programme for the Whole School*. Paul Chapman Publishing/SAGE.

Smutny, J. F., Walker, S. Y. and Meckstroth, E. A. (1997) *Teaching Young Gifted Children in the Regular Classroom: Identifying, Nuturing, and Challenging Ages 4–9*. Free Spirit Publishing.

South West Gifted and Talented Education (2008) *Engaging Pupil Voice in Gifted and Talented Education: Stepping with Students into their Spaces and Places.* Devon Learning and Development Partnership.

Stern, J. (2004) *Involving Parents.* Continuum.

Stevens, M. (2008) *Challenging the Gifted Child.* Jessica Kingsley.

Striker, S. and Kimmel, E. (1979) *The Anti-Colouring Book.* Hippo.

Sutherland, M. (2007) *Gifted and Talented in the Early Years.* Paul Chapman.

Teare, B. (1999) *Effective Resources for Able and Talented Children.* Network Educational Press

Teare, B. (2000a) *Effective Provision for Able and Talented Children.* Network Educational Press.

Teare, B. (2000b) *More Effective Resources for Able and Talented Children.* Network Educational Press.

Urban, K. and Jellen, H. (1996) *Tests for Creative Thinking: Drawing Production.* Harcourt Test Publishers.

Wallace, B., Cave, D. and Berry, A. (2008) *Teaching Problem Solving and Thinking Skills through Science.* Routledge.

Wallace, B., Leyden, S., Montgomery, D., Winstanley, C., Pomerantz, M. and Fitton, S. (2009) *Raising the Achievement of All Pupils within an Inclusive Setting: Practical Strategies for Developing Best Practice.* Routledge.

Wallace, B., Maker, J., Cave, D. and Chandler, S. (2004) *Thinking Skills and Problem Solving: An Inclusive Approach – A Practical Guide for Teachers in Primary Schools.* David Fulton.

White, M. (1993) *Circle Time in Schools.* David Fulton.

Young, P. and Tyre, C. (1992) *Gifted: Realising Children's Potential.* Open University Press.

Zohar, D. and Marshall, I. (2000) *SQ: Spiritual Intelligence, The Ultimate Intelligence.* Bloomsbury.

Index

W

Z

The Independent Thinking Series brings together some of the most innovative practitioners working in education today under the guidance of Ian Gilbert, founder of Independent Thinking Ltd. www.independentthinking.co.uk

The Big Book of Independent Thinking: Do things no one does or do things everyone does in a way no one does — Edited by Ian Gilbert
ISBN 978-190442438-3

Little Owl's Book of Thinking: An Introduction to Thinking Skills — Ian Gilbert
ISBN 978-190442435-2

The Little Book of Thunks: 260 questions to make your brain go ouch! — Ian Gilbert
ISBN 978-184590062-5

The Buzz: A practical confidence builder for teenagers — David Hodgson
ISBN 978-190442481-9

Essential Motivation in the Classroom — Ian Gilbert
ISBN 978-041526619-2

Are You Dropping the Baton?: How schools can work together to get transition right
— Dave Harris Edited by Ian Gilbert
ISBN 978-184590081-6

Leadership with a Moral Purpose: Turning Your School Inside Out — Will Ryan Edited by Ian Gilbert
ISBN 978-184590084-7

The Little Book of Big Stuff about the Brain — Andrew Curran Edited by Ian Gilbert
ISBN 978-184590085-4

Rocket Up Your Class!: 101 high impact activities to start, end and break up lessons — Dave Keeling Edited by Ian Gilbert
ISBN 978-184590134-9

www.independentthinking.co.uk   **www.crownhouse.co.uk**

The Independent Thinking Series brings together some of the most innovative practitioners working in education today under the guidance of Ian Gilbert, founder of Independent Thinking Ltd. www.independentthinking.co.uk

 The Lazy Teacher's Handbook: How Your Students Learn More When You Teach Less —
Jim Smith Edited by Ian Gilbert
ISBN 978-184590289-6

 **The Learner's Toolkit:** Developing Emotional Intelligence, Instilling Values for Life, Creating Independent Learners and Supporting the SEAL Framework for Secondary Schools —
Jackie Beere Edited by Ian Gilbert
ISBN 978-184590070-0

The Little Book of Charisma: Applying the Art and Science — David Hodgson Edited by Ian Gilbert
ISBN 978-184590293-3

The Little Book of Inspirational Teaching Activities: Bringing NLP into the Classroom —
David Hodgson Edited by Ian Gilbert
ISBN 978-184590136-3

 The Little Book of Music for the Classroom: Using Music to Improve Memory, Motivation, Learning and Creativity — Nina Jackson Edited by Ian Gilbert
ISBN 978-184590091-5

 The Little Book of Values: Educating children to become thinking, responsible and caring citizens — Julie Duckworth Edited by Ian Gilbert
ISBN 978-184590135-6

 The Primary Learner's Toolkit — Jackie Beere Edited by Ian Gilbert
ISBN 978-184590395-4

The Perfect (Ofsted) Lesson — Jackie Beere Edited by Ian Gilbert
ISBN: 978-184590460-9

www.independentthinking.co.uk　　　**www.crownhouse.co.uk**